AVERAGE JOE

Joseph Brozovich

Paperback-Press
an imprint of A & S Publishing
A & S Holmes, Inc.

ISBN 10: 1-945669-11-X
ISBN 13: 978-1945669118

DEDICATION

This book is dedicated to my wife Dawn and my children: Joanne, Joyce, Joe, Amy Michael and Danielle. I would also like to dedicate this book to my grandchildren: J.D., Cassandra, Mary, Jackson, Makayla, Emily and Aria. They were all kind enough to supply me with much of the material I needed to write this book.

Contents

INTRODUCTION

I wrote this book to describe what life was like being born in 1944 and growing up in Chicago in the 40s, 50s and 60s. In the 1960s, phase II of my life started when we got married and started having children. I dedicate this book to my six children and seven grandchildren. I wrote this book so that they could would know some of our family history and see the huge differences between the era in which I grew up and their own.

I called the book Average Joe because I always saw myself as a regular kid, nothing special. And since my parents named me Joe, I named the book Average Joe. In this book I recall some ordinary, unusual and exceptional things that happened in my lifetime. For instance, the reader can read my firsthand account of being stuck in the great Chicago Blizzard of 1967. They can also read about my team and I earning a U.S. patent for our piece of the Chicago 9-1-1 system. They can also read about the origins of voice mail.

I thought I should write this stuff down since I am the only family member left who knows most of our family history. Someday I will be gone and this family history will be lost to future generations. So here it is for all to enjoy. Everything is from my memory and my recollections of what my parents told me about their early lives before I was born. So it may not be 100% accurate but it's the best I can do with my 72 year old brain. I hope the readers enjoy reading it and if I am still around when you read it and you have any questions about it, please ask me. I may or may not know the answers but right now I am the oldest person you can ask.

CHAPTER 1 FAMILY HISTORY

The Story of Mary Peterlich

My mother, Mary Peterlich, was born in January of 1916 on a farm in Croatia in the region known as Lika. Her name is spelled Petrlic' in Croatian. She was one of eighteen children born of two mothers and one father. Her father's name was Mile Peterlich and her mother's name was Manda Hecimovich. See her birth certificate below. Notice that it is written in Croatian.

My grandmother died when my mom was just ten years old. About that time her father told her she was done with school and pulled her out of school to stay home and help out on the farm. He said women didn't need an education because all they had to do was stay home and have babies. So her formal education ended in fourth grade. That's why there are no graduation pictures of my mom anywhere.

Around 1937, my mom immigrated to the United States. My memory is a little shaky on this but I think she took a train or trains from Croatia to London, England. There she caught a boat from London to New York City. Once she got there she had to go to Ellis Island and go through the immigration process. She had to identify herself and then show them she had money to support herself. She said that her siblings gave her $100 for that purpose. I guess that money also paid for her food and transportation. I don't know what her $100 would be worth in today's money but I am guessing like over $1000.

After leaving Ellis Island, she took a train from New York City to Chicago where she met her brother John and/or sister Manda. That was a pretty good trip for a 21-year old girl who could only speak Croatian. When she got hungry on the boat, she would point to food other passengers had and they would bring her the items she identified. Once she arrived at her destination in Chicago, she started her job as a bar maid. Some of the time she worked for her brother in his place and other times she would work for her sister in her tavern. While at her sister's tavern, her side job was watching her sister Manda's daughters Julie, Josie, and Laurie. Julie was the oldest at about 13 when my mom arrived in Chicago.

The Story of Joe Brozovich

My father, Joe Brozovich, was born in the United States but both his parents were born in Croatia. So my brother and I were 100% Croatian even though we were born in the United States and never even been to Croatia. My dad's father was Paul (Leopold) Brozovich and his mother's maiden name was Mary (Maria) Lukas. My dad's baptism certificate states that he was born in Gary, Indiana on Nov. 1, 1913. See his baptism certificate below:

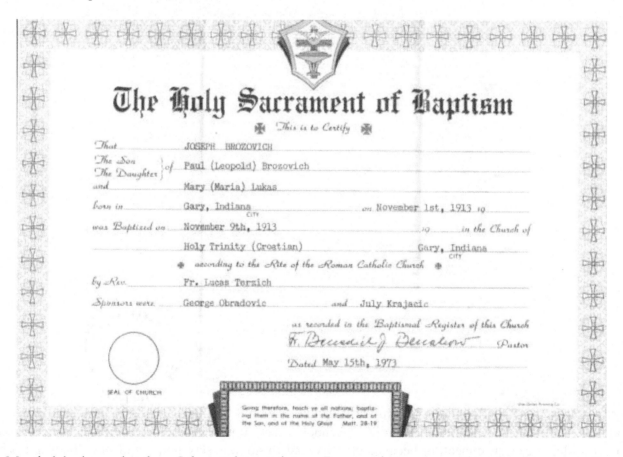

My dad had one brother, John, and two sisters, Rose and Anne. Another daughter passed away shortly after birth. That death basically caused my grandmother to have nervous breakdown and she was unable to care for her four living children including my dad. So my grandfather took his four children to his brother Jim who lived on the East Side of Chicago. My dad's Uncle Jim and his wife had no children of their own but raised my dad and his siblings. I think my dad went to Taylor School on the East Side. His graduation picture is shown below.

It looks like my dad is in the second row from the top, third kid from the left. This is the only graduation picture of my dad. His formal education ended when he graduated from grammar school. He was probably about thirteen years old when this picture was taken. At this point, he started looking for work. However, work was hard to get back then because this was shortly before the stock market crash in 1929 and the start of the Great Depression. One time I found my dad's diary for that time and read "Shoveled coal all day, made 35 cents".

I think around 1930 or 1931, my dad got a job at Youngstown Sheet and Tube Company in East Chicago, Indiana. My dad's job at the mill was a steel pourer. He controlled the flow of molten steel from a big caldron into ingot molds. When the molds cooled off some, they could be rolled into whatever thickness the customer needed. For instance, steel for car fenders would be thicker than steel for soup cans. My dad got his picture into a company book one year pouring steel. See that picture below. My dad is the one holding the long pole.

My dad worked shift work his entire career at Youngstown. One week he would work days from 7 a.m. to 3 p.m. The next week he would work evenings from 3 p.m. to 11 p.m. The last week he would work nights from 11p.m. to 7 a.m. He did this for 38 years until he retired. His job was very difficult. He had to stand for his entire shift and it was very hot there. He wore long underwear year round because the molten steel would often splash and pieces of it would hit him and burn holes in his clothes and skin. He would also sweat a lot because of the heat. However, his employer provided guys like my dad with salt tablets to help them hold some of the moisture in their bodies instead of sweating it all out. He said he sweated so much that he seldom had to go to the bathroom to urinate. The only good thing about this job was that it was one of the higher paid jobs in the mill. Unfortunately several people died in this area of the mill because it was an unsafe place to work especially when some workers came to work drunk resulting in fatal accidents. Actually, my dad had a heart attack when he was in his 50s and the mill gave him an easier job so he did that for the last few years before he retired.

When I was attending Purdue University, I interned at Youngstown for the summers before my junior and senior years in college. One week I was in the Safety department and we had to investigate two on-the-job deaths. This was a really unsafe place to work. Hopefully, when OSHA (occupational Safety and Health Administration) came into existence, the jobs got safer but my dad and I never saw the improvements but I do remember seeing rats in the mill as big as cats.

When I was going to college, my dad told me that if college ever got too hard, he could get me a job in the mill. I told him "Dad, it will never get that hard" and it never did.

My father had three living siblings, a brother named John, a sister named Rose and another sister named Anne. His brother John married a lady named Mary Cookich, had three children (I think) and spent his life on the East Side and Hegwisch, the community just south of the East Side. His sister Rose got married to a guy named Wagner, had four children, and lived on the East Side till she died. My dad's sister Anne got married to a man named Shamnick, had ten kids and lived her life on the East Side. She was the first of my dad's siblings to pass away.

My aunts and uncles had many children who were my cousins. However, we didn't associate with them very much. When we were small, we attended several birthday parties with them but once we started high school we went our own ways and did not have much to do with any of them. My brother and I both left the East Side after we got married and never returned except to visit our parents.

Joe and Mary Get Married

While tending bar for her brother John or sister Manda, my mom met my dad who apparently was a frequent customer of the bar. Both siblings owned taverns and my mom earned her keep by tending bar. When she moved from one tavern to another, my dad followed her to the other tavern. He apparently asked about her when he didn't see her at the former bar, and he was told the location of the other bar. They hit it off and were married in 1942.

Before my parents got married, my mom got a job at the University of Chicago working in the kitchen. There were lots of young men there preparing for their roles in the World War II war effort. She lived in a small apartment with her new found friend Mary Barica. You will see Mary's name on their Marriage Certificate. My dad's brother John was his best man and his name is also shown on the Marriage Certificate.

Notice the name of the church on the Marriage Certificate: "Sacred Heart Croatian Church". I find it interesting that they left off the fact that it was a Roman Catholic Church but they didn't omit the word "Croatian". It is my understanding that when immigrants came from Europe (the Old Country) to the USA, they initially came to live with their friends and relatives. In most cases those friends and relatives came from the same region in Europe. So this neighborhood in the city of Chicago was populated by Croatians like my parents. St. George Church, which is where my parents spent most of their time, was a Slovenian Catholic Church.

So when the immigrants needed a church, the people built their own Catholic churches. So even when I was growing up, one of the Sunday masses commemorated the people who built the church by giving the homily in their native language. This made it hard for me to appreciate because the Mass was said in Latin and the homily at St. George was in Slovenian. I couldn't understand anything!! However, this was only for one of the Sunday masses. Needless to say, I never went to that mass again. I discussed this practice with a friend of mine who grew up in St. Louis and he said the same thing happened there. Each nationality built and attended their own churches. When I attended a Catholic mass in Miami

Florida, the entire mass was in Spanish.

My parents told me that the immigrants were very clannish. If you were a Polish guy, you were expected to marry a Polish girl and have more Polish kids. However, if a Polish guy married an Italian girl, they would both be excommunicated from their families. Fortunately, by the time my brother and I got married to our wives, no one cared about the nationalities of the bride and groom. My first wife's parents were Polish and Czechoslovakian. So my first five kids are 50% Croatian and 25% Polish and 25% Czechoslovakian.

In May of 1944, my mom became a U.S. citizen. She could have become a citizen by virtue of the fact that she married my dad, but she chose to do it the hard way. She studied for and passed the naturalization test and she became a full-fledged citizen of the USA. Her naturalization paper is shown below. She kept this paper till the day she died.

CHAPTER 2 MY EARLY CHILDHOOD

Life Begins for Joe Brozovich

I was born Joseph Michael Brozovich in Chicago in September of 1944. Before I was born, my mom and dad were living in his Uncle Jim's house on the southeast side of Chicago. However, when my mom got pregnant with me, she insisted that they get their own place and so they did.

My earliest memories of my childhood go back to around the time my brother John was born in March of 1949. We were living in a one bedroom apartment owned by the family of my soon to be best friend, Joe Hrstich. His dad owned the three story building we lived in. His family lived on the first floor. They rented the second and third floors. The third floor was divided into two small apartments with a door between them. We lived in the back apartment. Joe Hrstich and I got to be great friends. He was just nine months older than me but we obviously had a lot in common. We were both 100% Croatian and proud of it. Our moms also became best friends. Both our dads worked in Steel Mills but they were different mills. My dad worked at the Youngstown Sheet and Tube Company in East Chicago, Indiana and Joe Hrstich's dad worked at U.S. Steel just about a mile south of us in Illinois.

The one thing I learned from my dad was to work hard and save your money for the things you want. He lived those words by his work in the steel mill. As I recall, my dad's union went on strike almost every time their contract came up for renewal. That was about every three years. That meant that my dad got no pay check for the duration of the strike. That was because no one would hire strikers because they knew they would quit as soon as the strike was settled. Once, a strike lasted around 6 months. This occurred while Eisenhower was president. The president finally invoked the Taft-Hartley Act and forced the strikers to meet with the company personnel and resolve the strike and they did. The amazing thing about this time in my life was that my parents always paid their bills and put food on the table. I remember going shopping with them for groceries. First they went to the bank to withdraw the money they needed. Then they would go shopping and buy the sale items at each store. This pattern of living showed me that I better save some money each month so that if I ever lost my job, I could still feed my family. We never went hungry but I do remember that one time we had corn on the cob for dinner. There was no meat or potatoes, just corn on the cob. I guess it was on sale that week. My brother and I loved it. We didn't even complain about it.

Life on the East Side of Chicago

Our lives revolved around our families, our friends, and our church. Most of those people lived on the East Side of Chicago. The East Side is one of 77 neighborhoods in the city of Chicago. The boundaries of the East Side are Lake Michigan on the east, the Calumet River on the west, and Eggers Grove and Wolfe Lake Park on the south. The north boundary is where the Calumet River fed into Lake Michigan. We were cut off from the rest of Chicago by the Calumet River. However, there were several draw bridges that connected the East Side to the rest of Chicago.

World War II was still going on when I was born but my dad was not able to serve in the military because he was in a car accident before the war that caused some permanent problems. So he was exempt from serving in the military. I think my folks were waiting to get married until he was either done serving or until they found out he couldn't serve.

During most of WWII, I was not yet born but I suspect that my dad was working lots of overtime at the mill to make steel products needed for the war effort. They wanted to buy a house but my dad didn't want to get a mortgage because he lost his first car when he was unable to make the payments when he lost his job. So they waited until they could pay cash for their first (and only) home.

By 1950, my parents had saved up enough money to buy the house on Avenue M. My father lived there until his death in 1974 and my mom lived there until she moved to Missouri in 1999. So she lived in that house for 49 years. While living there, my parents met their next door neighbors Mitzie and Ed and their two sons Eddie and Bobby. My mom and Mitzie got to be great friends. They would often talk by opening the windows facing each other's houses and talking through the windows' and across the narrow gangway between their houses.

Living on Avenue M and Going to St. George School (SGS)

After we moved into our new 100 year old house on Avenue M, I started first grade at St. George School, only two blocks away from our house. They just finished building the school and I was in the first class to attend all eight years of grammar school there.

The school was run by nuns headed by the principal, Sister Bertha. Some of the nuns were nice but some were very strict. The school was crowded with some classrooms holding two grades like 5th and 6th. I remember there being over 40 kids in one of my classrooms. Some of the nuns would literally beat up the kids when they misbehaved. I remember one nun beating up a kid at his desk with her fists while he tried to cover his head with his hands. If you dared to tell your parents that you got a beating from a nun, they would agree with her and finish the job at home. Life was tough back then but we learned to listen to the nuns and keep our mouths shut unless we were called on to speak in class.

When I started in first grade at St. George School, I had no friends because I spent the first six years of my life about 12 blocks south of St. George School. The other kids knew each other because they lived in the same neighborhood before they started attending school there. So a big gang of them took great joy in chasing me home almost every night. They never hurt me but it was still a pain. One time while chasing me home, I ran through some yards and between some garages and noticed that only one of them was chasing me. So I turned and ran straight at him. I knocked him down and jumped on his chest and pounded him with my fists. A funny thing happened after that incident. They stopped chasing me. I actually made friends with some of them over time.

I met a new friend named Albert. He was in the same boat I was in being another new kid at the school. I guess he was treated just like I was. So we became friends. He was being raised by his grandparents because his parents never married. In fact, I don't think he ever met his real dad. Needless to say, his grandfather was very strict with him.

Being a Catholic school, all students were required to attend mass every day. Attending mass was hard because the mass was offered in Latin and there was no homily for weekday masses. Albert and I started hanging out together during mass time and we would show up just as the students were leaving church and heading to school. One time we got caught in some guy's garage and that was the end of playing hooky from mass.

Saint George School

One day, when school was not in session, I was doing some chores for the nun in our classroom. The nun had to leave but told me to rearrange the desks before I left. I guess the nuns got tired of looking at the same faces in the same places so they would move the desks around a few times a year just because. So I put my desk in the last row of the room between the two prettiest girls in the class. When all the kids returned to school, everyone had to find their desks. I played dumb and ultimately found my desk exactly where I put it. For the next several months I enjoyed my new desk neighbors. I think I also had the good sense to move the troublesome kids' desks away from mine so I didn't have to worry about them copying off me or bothering me in class. The nun never mentioned anything to me about the location of the desks and I never told anyone what I did.

There is a lesson to be learned in this story. Whenever an opportunity presents itself, take full advantage of it because you never know if you will ever get the same chance again.

Joe and the Seventh Grade Reading Contest

Life was fairly uneventful through grades one through six. Along the way, I learned that I was good at math and could finish my homework ahead of everyone else. Then things got interesting when I got into seventh grade. There was a book reading contest that year. Each of us got a map of the US and each time we read a book and turned in a book report, we got a new state sticker to put on our map. Back then, all you needed was 48 state stickers to completely fill up the map since Alaska and Hawaii did not become states until 1959. Well I took that as a personal challenge and over the course of the book contest, I read 70 books. I read the entire series of Hardy boys' mystery books, all the Nancy Drew books, and many other books. There was a series of books in our school library which talked about famous people when they were kids. The books were about George Washington, Abraham Lincoln, Daniel Boone, Davey Crockett and many others. I also read that entire series. Sometimes I would read a whole book in one night. I think I really liked those books because the heroes of the stories were young kids like me. By the time I finished the contest, I had added Canada, Mexico and many islands to my map so I got credit for all 70 of the books I read. Apparently, the competition was the key to my success.

Joe and John Become Altar Boys

When I got to seventh grade, I was asked if I wanted to be an altar boy. I said sure and they gave me as list of prayers to memorize in Latin. While I was working on them at home, my brother John heard me and he also learned the prayers. So when I recited the Latin prayers for the nuns, my brother did too and we both became altar boys in spite of the fact that John was only in second grade at the time. So we served many morning masses together. I think the earliest mass was at 6 am or possibly 6.30 a.m. My mom would wake us up early and we would go and serve mass before school started. Somehow we didn't mind getting up early and going to mass before school. We remained altar boys together until I started high school.

CHAPTER 3 GROWING UP WITH MARY AS MY MOM

Mary was a Stay-at-Home Mom

Whenever I think about my mom, I think of her always working on something. She had a regular schedule for every week. On Monday, she would wash clothes. On Tuesday she would iron clothes since everything we wore back then was cotton. Wednesday may have been for baking. Another day of the week would be for cleaning house. She had something major to do every day of the week. She wouldn't sit down to rest or watch TV until after dinner was finished. Even when she finally sat down, she would darn socks or knit or crochet or doing something else with her hands. I don't think she ever just rested without doing anything.

Joe Brozovich Senior 1913-1974

On March 4, 1974, I got a call at work from the Chicago Police Department. They told me that my dad was involved in a car crash. I asked if he was okay. They told me he died. I was devastated. I had just seen him a couple of weeks ago and he was fine. Now he was dead at the age of 60.

I found out from my mom that my dad had gone to the doctor recently and the doctor said my dad was doing so well that he took him took him off of his blood pressure medicine, nitroglycerin. On that day my dad drove his car to Calumet Park on Lake Michigan to see if the fish were biting. As he was driving his car, he must have had a heart attack because he made a big U-turn and crashed his car into the corner of a building. By the time the Emergency Medical team arrived, he was dead.

My mom's best friend went to the hospital and identified my dad's body. Now my mom was a widow at the age of 58. She never learned how to drive a car and the only car they had was totaled in the crash.

Fortunately for my mom, she had lots of friends and they took care of her. Her friends and neighbors took her shopping for groceries. When the weather was bad, they took her to church with them. When the weather was nice she could walk to neighborhood grocery stores to buy a few small items she could carry by herself. When she had doctor appointments, she could take a city bus if no one was able to drive her there.

After my dad died, she lived in her house on the East Side by herself from 1974 to 1999, a total of 25 years. All told, she lived in that house 49 years from 1950 to 1999. She took care of her house, paid her bills and managed her money by herself. In 1999, we moved her to Springfield, Missouri to be with me and my family.

Mary and her Faith

Mom was a devout Roman Catholic. Her life revolved around her church. She went to church every Sunday and holy day. She would have to be deathly ill to miss mass on a Sunday and it seldom, if ever, happened. After my dad died in 1974, my mom attended mass every day.

Whenever her church had a bake sale, rummage sale, or any other fund raising event, they could always count on my Mary to be there. On some Sundays, the ladies of the parish served the men's club breakfast and my mom was always there, helping in any way she could. She might be seen cooking, serving food or just cleaning up the kitchen.

When they needed volunteers to clean the church, my mom was there with her bucket, scrub brush and mop. The ladies of St. George parish kept that church looking beautiful all the time. St. George Church celebrated their 75th and their 100th anniversaries while my mom was attending there.

Once, when my mom was visiting with us in Missouri for Christmas, she returned home to find that she had no heat in her house. No heat in your house in January in Chicago is a very bad thing. Her hot water heating system froze and all her pipes and her toilet broke. Guess what she did? She went to the rectory where the parish priest lived and asked him to help her. He immediately found another member of the parish who volunteered to take her in while her house was being fixed. She stayed with this lady for several weeks while all the radiators and pipes in her house were replaced.

The ladies of the parish elected my mom Mother of the Year twice. She was Mother of the year for us every year.

I guess my mom's faith convinced my brother and I that we should also be loyal members of our respective churches and that's exactly what happened.

Mom and Her Homemade Apple Strudel

What I remember most about my mom was her homemade apple strudel. She would go buy apples when they were in season and on sale in the local grocery stores. When the day came to make the strudel, the first thing she would do is peel the apples and slice them into small thin slices. Then she would create and knead a big ball of dough about the size of a 16 inch softball. She would then roll the dough until it was as thin as she could make it. It looked like a big skinny pancake. Then she would slowly and meticulously stretch that dough until it covered her entire rectangular kitchen table. I swear the dough was paper thin. Before doing that she put a big white table cloth on the table. Then she would sprinkle the apple slices on the stretched dough along with some cinnamon and sugar. She would then pick up one end of the table cloth and use it to roll the dough with the apples inside into a log about three to four feet long. Then she would put the log onto a baking pan in the shape of the letter "S". She would then put it into the oven and bake it for about an hour or just put it in the freezer until she decided to bake it. After my dad died, she always had about a dozen strudels in her freezer just waiting to be baked. Whenever I called her to tell I was coming to see her, she would pop one of those strudels in the oven and bake it. When I arrived, the strudel would be done and the whole house smelled like baked apples. She entered her strudel in a baking contest on the East Side and won first prize. She got her picture in the local paper holding one of her strudels. Years later when we tried to make her strudel recipe, we realized that the amount of ingredients needed for the strudel was just the right amount to cover her own kitchen table with the stretched dough. If the table anyone else used was too big or too small, the strudel did not turn out right. She often gave other people her strudels so all they had to do was bake the strudel and eat it. This was one of her favorite gifts for people. She would also donate them when there was a party, or a wedding, or a funeral, or a church function that included food. All the members of her church loved my mom's strudel and it was always the first dessert to be eaten.

My mom was a great baker. She also made Walnut Bread that was equally good but she only made it for Christmas and Easter. She also won first prize in a local contest for her home-made walnut bread. It was yummy too but not as good as the strudel in my book.

On one occasion my wife and our family went to Door County Wisconsin on a vacation and we bought some fresh cherries and brought them home to my mom. We asked her if she could make a cherry strudel. She obliged but I still thought the apple strudel was better. My brother John liked her cheese strudel better than the apple strudel but apple was always the best kind in my book.

On another occasion, the mayor of Chicago sent a team of city dignitaries including Fire Commissioner Quinn to St. George School to see one of the first schools in the city of Chicago with a fire alarm system. This was a big deal then because a total of 92 students and three nuns died in a fire at Our Lady of the Angels School in Chicago on December 1, 1958. The school had no fire alarm system, no sprinkler system and no smoke detectors because smoke detectors did not become commercially available until 1969.

The city dignitaries who came to St. George were treated to some coffee and treats including my mom's apple strudel. One of the dignitaries, possibly commissioner Quinn, asked the ladies there who made the strudel. The ladies said my mom did. He said he wanted to meet the "strudel maker". So they took him to the kitchen to meet my mom. He complemented her on her strudel and his complement was one of the highlights of her life. She often spoke of that day.

In 1984 my mom entered her strudel in a park district baking contest and she won first prize with her strudel. However, I didn't realize that her winning the Chicago Park District area automatically qualified her to enter the 1984 citywide Bake-O-Rama contest which included 20 city parks. Mom won first place in the coffee-cake division. See her picture below holding her prize winning apple strudel. Mom is the lovely lady on the far right. I always knew her apple strudel was great but I never would have guessed she would win a citywide baking contest.

East Siders Stephanie Golob (left) and Mary Brozovich (right) treated Calumet Park arts and craft instructor Betty Inglimo (center) to a plate of their recent 'blue ribbon' baked goodies.

CHAPTER 4 LIFE IN CHICAGO

Growing up in Chicago

Chicago was a wonderful safe city when we were growing up. When we were in grammar school and high school we would think nothing of catching a CTA (Chicago Transit Authority) bus and taking a journey to downtown Chicago, Comiskey (White Sox) Park, Wrigley (Cubs) Field, Soldier's Field, Lincoln Park, Riverview amusement park, the International Amphitheater or anywhere else within the city limits of Chicago. We went to the International Amphitheater to see wrestling matches. We went downtown to see first-run movies or go to the public library there or go to the Chicago Chess Club. All the action was downtown because there were no malls back then. So if you wanted to see the latest movie or shop in the best stores, you had to go downtown. We never worried about being robbed or getting into any trouble along the way.

About the time I got into fifth grade at St. George School, I decided to be a paperboy. So I delivered daily and Sunday copies of the now defunct Chicago Herald American newspaper to four consecutive blocks of customers. Each week I got a bill from the guy who ran the news agency. I was required to collect money from the people I delivered the papers to. My pay was the difference between what I collected and the bill I got from the agency. My pay averaged about $7 per week. That was big money when a decent allowance was 25 or 50 cents a week. I even became an honor carrier one week and had my picture in the paper. See that picture and article below:

Honor Carrier Boy

If you want to know how to plan for the future, just ask Joseph M. Brozovich Jr., 14, today's CHICAGO AMERICAN honor carrier boy. He'll tell you:

"Buy bonds!"

That's what he is doing to insure his college education. He hopes to attend Purdue University and study engineering. He explained:

"I am interested in engineering because I like to figure out difficult problems dealing with arithmetic."

Joseph is a freshman at St. Francis de Sales High School. His favorite subjects are math, Spanish and world history.

In grade school, at St. George, he was honored for having read more books in one semester than any other student.

The Brozovich family lives at 9731 Avenue M.

Young Joseph delivers THE AMERICAN to 32 families in his community, daily and Sunday. With his earnings from his newspaper job, he buys U. S. Savings bonds. He'll keep saving bonds, he says, until he has enough to afford college.

Joseph works out of Branch 33, at 9753 Avenue L, where Emil Santelli is the distributor.

When I got paid, I went straight to the store that sold comic books. I would buy comic books every single week. I bought comics about Donald Duck, Superman, Archie, Little Lulu, War stories, and Classic Comics which had stories like "A Tale of Two Cities", "From the Earth to the Moon", "20,000 Leagues Under the Sea", and more.

When I asked my parents for a new bike, they told me to save my money and buy it for myself. So I did. I saved up $40 for a new bike. I went to get it with my dad and he helped me bring it into the house. I had to assemble part of it like mounting the tires and handle bars but I was beaming with pride by the time I finished. I filled the tires with air using my dad's air pump and took my brand new bike for a spin. It rode like a dream. That night I remember going down to the basement and just staring at my new bike. It was mine all mine. I paid every penny for it including the tax.

Being a Teenager in Chicago in the 1950s

I remember some of the main things I did while growing up on the East Side. Often I would go play on the swings and slides and monkey bars at Pietrowski's Playground, affectionately known as Dago Park due to the large Italian population in that area. (Incidentally, the Internet says a Dago is a highly offensive racial slur for an Italian.) Dago Park was only a half a block from our house. We also played 16 inch softball there and on the side streets. People drove carefully and we would move whenever a car turned into the street we were playing on. I guess 16 inch softball was invented in Chicago. Most places use 12 inch balls. The nice thing about 16 inch soft balls is when they get pretty well used, they are soft as pillows. So when the ball hit a car window for example, there was never any damage because the ball was so soft it couldn't hurt anything. However, that wasn't true when the ball was new. Then it was hard as a rock.

One time we were playing in a vacant lot, down the street from my house what I hit a long home run right into the basement window of house that backed up to the vacant lot. I went to the house and told the people who lived there that I broke their window. They were okay with it but they wanted me to fix it. So I measured the window and my dad and I went to the hardware store and got a piece of glass with the right dimensions. My dad removed the old glass and tried to put in the new piece but it was too small. I neglected to account for the caulk. So we went back to the hardware store and got another piece of glass. This time it was the right size and my dad taught me how to replace a window pane.

Fun at Calumet Park

Another one of my favorite activities was going to Calumet (Cal) Park which was about six blocks from our house and right on Lake Michigan. We could swim in Lake Michigan or play baseball or football or just ride our bikes all over the park. We even played on the monkey bars. Swimming in Lake Michigan was our favorite summer activity. When the wind was blowing toward the shore, all the floating junk like popcorn slag, dead fish, etc., would find its way into our swimming area. The water was nice and warm and dirty. Some days the wind would blow the water and trash back out into the lake. Then the water was crystal clear. With our snorkeling goggles, we could probably see 5 whole feet in front of us under the water. Unfortunately, when the wind was blowing everything out to sea, the warm water was also blown away from shore and the water was freezing cold. One time I remember the lifeguards' station posted the water temperature as 56 degrees. Brrrr.

Oftentimes, when my dad worked days from 7am to 3p.m., he would take my brother and I to Cal park to play baseball after work. He would hit the ball to us and, if we caught it, we would get points: 100 pts for a fly ball, 50 points for one bounce or 25 points for a ground ball. The first one to get 500 points won. If you missed a fly ball for example, you would lose the 100 pts from your current score. When someone won, you would just yell that you won and start the next game. The game was kind of like playing fetch with a dog and we were the dogs. We didn't care. We had fun and got lots of good exercise. I am sure my brother and I slept well the nights we played 500 baseball with our dad.

Watching Wrestling Matches

At that time in our lives, we were big professional wrestling fans. We thought the matches were real. We watched our heroes on Saturday afternoons on TV and then again at midnight from Bridgeport, Connecticut. These matches ended at 2:00 a.m. Sunday morning. It was really hard for me to stay up and watch the best match starting about 1:45 a.m. Then I had to get up for mass the next morning. Life was hard for a kid in the 50s.

We even went to see live wrestling matches at the International Amphitheater on 47th and Halstead. I vaguely remember the matches starting at 7 or 8 p.m. on a weekend night. So my friend Joe Hrstich and I would take the three buses to get to the place before the matches started. On one occasion, we waited at the back door for the wrestlers to come out after the matches were over. They came out and we walked with them to their cars. Some of them even gave us autographed pictures. That was a real big deal for us then.

After the matches were over, we would return home with the same three buses around midnight. The amazing thing was we never had a problem with anyone bothering us even though we were standing outside waiting for busses after midnight in neighborhoods where problems could occur and definitely would today.

1955 Wisconsin Vacation

My best friend Joe Hrstich's family owned a cabin in northern Wisconsin. They got it so they could go there in the summer when Joe Hrstich's mother's allergies were awful. One year we were invited to visit them there. My dad had to work but he took my mom, brother and I to the train station in downtown Chicago and sent us off on our adventure. We took the train to Rice Lake, Wisconsin. From there we caught a bus that took us to Winter, Wisconsin. Joe Hrstich's brother Bob picked us up there and drove us to their cabin. I think the cabin was about seven miles from Winter, Wisconsin. It was a nice little cabin but it was in the middle of nowhere. Bob drove back to Chicago leaving us up there without a car. It didn't matter since none of us drove anyway. The cabin was also missing a couple other things we kind of got used to in Chicago like running water and a phone. So we got water from an outside well and we used an outhouse in the woods. The nearest neighbor had a phone in case of an emergency. Fortunately, we never had an emergency that required a phone.

We got our food from a guy who had a truck and drove around the area bringing food and other small items to folks like us who couldn't get to a city with stores. This actually worked quite well. The moms cooked and we played outside during the day and played board games at night. We didn't have a TV either and if we did, I doubt that it could receive anything where we were.

Once we decided to build a fort out of real wood. We managed to chop down about half a dozen trees with an old dull axe we found. We figured out real fast that we were not going to live long enough to chop down enough trees to build anything significant. So we abandoned the fort idea. Joe Hrstich later told me that his dad chopped up the trees we cut down and used them for firewood.

During the summer days, the temperatures got into the 90s. It was really hot and there was no air-conditioning. None the less, we played outside chasing little frogs around his property. Then we would catch the frogs and let them go and catch them again. Life is tough without electronic devices to play with.

At night the temperatures got down to freezing. I thought it was amazing how much the outside temperature varied during the course of the day. I was used to living next to Lake Michigan and it kept the air at a fairly constant temperature but there were no lakes that size where we were.

At night and sometimes during rainy days, we played board games. Monopoly was the game of choice most days. My friend Joe Hrstich was the all time Monopoly champion. I think he won most, if not all, of the games we played. Even when my brother and I conspired to beat him, it never worked and Joe always won. That was really boring.

After a few weeks in the north woods, my dad drove up to bring us home. I made him a map of how to find us and he said it led him right to us. He stayed with us a couple of days but eventually, he had to leave to get back to working in the mill.

But before he left, he had to try and do a little fishing. We went to some small lake and tried our luck. If it wasn't for bad luck we wouldn't have had any luck at all. I vaguely remember us catching a few small fish but nothing larger than a charm for his key chain.

Since Joe Hrstich's place was over 400 miles from Chicago, we left early one day to make it home in one day. That was before Interstate highways were invented so the only roads we could take were roads that connected cities together. We could go pretty fast on the open roads, but once we hit a city we were stuck in city traffic with stop lights and stop signs. Fortunately, the cities were small compared to Chicago. Finally we got home safe and sound from our big adventure.

We got our First TV

I remember us getting our first TV sometime in the 1950s. Back then, a TV was a piece of furniture with nice polished wood cabinet all around the electronics. The really nice ones had a radio and record player in them along with the TV. I guess they cost a fortune because the wood cabinets were really nice and all the electronics wasn't cheap when it first came out. All we ever had was a basic TV. Wireless remotes were not invented yet so kids were used to change the channels and adjust the volume.

Our TV was the best thing that ever happened to us except for the fact that it was in the shop about as much as it was in our house. Back then, TVs used electron tubes in all their circuits. The picture was even displayed on a big tube. The problem with tubes was that they were very hot when the TV was on and so they would eventually wear out and had to be replaced. From an electronic perspective, the characteristics of the tubes changed with age and so the TVs came with knobs in the front to control things like horizontal hold, vertical hold, vertical sync and more. Sometimes you could make some adjustments with those knobs that would correct the problems caused by the aging tubes and get a picture you could see again. However, you eventually needed to replace the tubes if you wanted a picture and sound on the TV. When I got old enough, I would pull the tubes out of the TV set and take them to a place that sold tubes and had a tube tester that the customers could use to test their own tubes. This was a hit or miss proposition. I remember one time I took the tubes to an electronics store and the tester told me all the tubes were bad. So I took them to another store to get a second opinion (hopefully a cheaper opinion). That store said about half of them were bad. I couldn't understand how the TV worked perfectly the day before and now suddenly, half the tubes went bad while the TV was turned off during the night. Thankfully, the electron tubes are all gone now and we don't have to replace or repair TVs nearly as much as we did back in the 1950s.

Playing Board Games

Among the many board games I played with my best friend Joe Hrstich were Monopoly, Clue, Scrabble, Checkers, and Chess. I liked checkers and chess the best because the outcome was based on performance and not chance. In games like Monopoly, you can win or lose depending on a roll of the dice. Whereas in checkers and chess, there is no element of chance such as rolling dice, drawing a card, or spinning a wheel like in other games. I also liked checkers for that reason. Checkers was one of my favorite games until my friend Joe Hrstich introduced me to Chess and I loved it. Joe Hrstich and I played many games together. We even went to the Chicago Chess club in downtown Chicago to play some of the best players in Chicago. We usually lost but we still loved playing. Chess became a big part of my life as the reader will see in subsequent chapters of this book.

Model Railroading

Another big pastime in the 1950s was model railroading. One Christmas, I got a brand new LIONEL® train set. I loved it. One I connected the tracks in the shape of a circle or oval, I was ready to go. Then I put the engine and all the cars on the tracks and coupled them together. Unfortunately, it got pretty boring watching the train going around in a big circle over and over again. So what people did back then was create a layout of something like a small city with a train running through it. In retrospect, the train layout was a money pit. I started out by getting a 4 foot by 8 foot piece of plywood and mounting it on a couple of saw horses in our basement. Then the work and spending began. I bought little plastic buildings for my "town". I got a train station for my train to stop at. I got light poles that had real lights in them. I also bought more railroad cars, track and two electric switches so that I had a couple of paths for my train to take. One of the neighbor kids sold me his train set for $10 so now I had a new engine and more cars to play with. Life was good.

Unfortunately, a 4 x 8 piece of plywood can only hold so much stuff and mine was pretty full and our basement was small and my dad got tired of looking at my train set in the middle of the basement. So we took my train set up to attic where all our old toys went to die. I set it up in the attic and got everything to work. Then I left it up there because it was too hot up there in the summertime to be up there. Sometimes I would go up to the attic and plug in my train set and watch it go around the tracks for a while but as I got older, the attraction faded. When I graduated from college and got married and moved away, my parents asked me to take the train set with me which I did. I took everything except the plywood.

When my kids were growing up and I had my own house, we would put the train up under the Christmas tree and watch it make endless circles around the base of the tree. When I got a pool table for my basement, I setup the train on the pool table and we watched it go around and around. But my kids got older and tired of the trains and I eventually sold my two trains, tracks, switches, buildings, etc. for $1200 to some collector in the 1990s. My mom told me she paid $50 for the original set they gave me so I guess I made a nice profit on it but I never tried to add up the costs of all the stuff that went into my model train layout.

In conclusion to my train escapades I wanted to add that my friend Joe Hrstich also had a model train set in his basement and we often compared notes about our respective train layouts. I think we were subconsciously having a competition to see who would have the best layout. I don't know who, if anyone, won that competition but I do know that it cost a lot of money to compete. I think the big winner was the guy who sold us all the stuff. The big department stores encouraged us model railroaders by putting up huge model railroad layouts at Christmas time. The Museum of Science and Industry had a fabulous layout with multiple trains and lots of buildings and just about everything you could ever have in train layout.

Joe Goes Bowling

The first time I went bowling was sometime in the 50s. I went to a 4 lane bowling alley in the back of a local tavern in the East Side business district around 106th and Ewing Avenue. It was so primitive that they had teenagers setting the pins. They didn't have to work very hard when I was bowling since I seldom hit any pins. I only remember my score for one game and that was a 31. However, I did give the gutters a good cleaning that day.

After bowling such a good score, I started to like bowling. There was another bowling alley on the East Side called Roll-A-Line and it had eight alleys and automatic pin setters. Sometimes my brother and I or my friends and I would go there and play. I eventually got so good, I could occasionally break

100. Back then a single game was either 25 or 50 cents so money was no object for a successful entrepreneur (paperboy) like me making a whole $7 a week.

While in high school I continued my amateur bowling career. Every Saturday morning, my brother John and I would take two buses to a bowling alley in South Chicago. I vaguely remember that it had about 24 alleys. We went there because games were cheap, like 25 cents each. Neither one of us was very good at bowling. I think I won most games because I was four and a half years older than John and a little stronger. I am sure there were some upsets by him as well. I imagine my bowling scores went up a little but not much.

My cousin Josie's husband passed away in the 1950s and she asked if I wanted his bowling ball. I said sure and from that day on I had my own bowling ball and bag. I even invested in my own pair of bowling shoes. So now I could walk in a bowling alley, put on my own shoes and polish my ball like the big guys on TV did. My scores gradually creeped over 100 and I was very happy with myself. I would occasionally send letters to my cousin Josie thanking her for the ball and telling her about my most recent high score. I still wasn't very good at bowling but at least I looked like a good bowler walking in the place with my own ball.

On one of our Saturday bowling junkets, two kids came up to us and asked us for money while we were waiting for the bus to go home. I didn't see any weapons and I recognized one kid from my high school. I even knew his name. The kid with him looked like his younger brother. So as far as I could see, the worst thing that could happen is that we might get into a fair fight with them and have a 50-50 chance of winning. I even had my bowling ball to use as a weapon if I needed it. So I told them to get lost and leave us alone. They looked like they didn't know what to do because I guess most people just gave them money. Fortunately, the bus showed up about then and we got on the bus and our altercation ended without incident.

On a few occasions my dad decided to come bowling with me and my brother. We went to another bowling alley near our house that had like 32 lanes. My dad really didn't know how to bowl so I gave him a few pointers, after all I was breaking a hundred most of the time now. I don't remember my dad's scores but I think they were close to mine. He threw the ball very hard and when he hit anywhere near the pocket, the pins exploded like they got hit with a hand grenade. One day after bowling my dad's arm hurt. So he went to the doctor and the doctor told him that something he was doing while bowling was causing the problem with his arm. Since he needed both arms to do his job at the mill, he decided to give up bowling with us. His only comment was "It's too bad I can't bowl anymore. I was starting to get good at it."

CHAPTER 5 HIGH SCHOOL MEMORIES

Life at St. Francis de Sales (SFDS) High School

In June of 1958 I graduated from St. George School. There were 23 kids in my graduating class. That fall I became a freshman at St. Francis de Sales High School located on 102nd and Ewing Avenue which was about six blocks from my house and about six blocks from St. George. Only a handful of my classmates from St. George went to St. Francis. My friend Albert went there for his first semester but then he had to transfer to Chicago Vocational School (CVS). I think his family just couldn't afford St. Francis. On a positive note, Al went to CVS while Dick Butkus was there. Butkus became an All-Pro linebacker for the Chicago Bears in the 60s.

My four years at St. Francis de Sales High School went by so fast it seemed like school was over before it started.

Students going to St. Francis de Sales had to make a decision on what courses to take. Student had two choices: college-prep or business. College-prep courses were designed to prepare the students for college while the business courses were there for people who did not intend to go to college. Those courses were like Typing, Shorthand, Home Economics, Bookkeeping, etc. Mostly girls took those courses to prepare them to for jobs like secretaries. Since I was planning to go to college, I am pretty sure I took all the college-prep courses offered by SFDS. Those courses included Algebra, Plane and Solid Geometry, Trigonometry, Biology, Physics, Mechanical Drawing, etc. All students were required to take English, Civics, Religion, Physical Education, Sociology, and History. I may have missed a few, but I think I named most of the important ones.

Our grades were numeric and not letter grades. For example, instead of giving me an A in a particular course, I got a numeric grade like 95.6 and everyone knew that an A was 92.0 and above. By some miracle, I think most of my grades were A's. After finishing high school, I came back one day to find out my class rank which was requested of me in college. I went to the office and asked at the office where exactly did I end up in my class of 130 students. I was surprised to find out that I graduated 3rd in my class. I guess all that hard work paid off.

Around the time I started high school, I was promoted to office boy in the newspaper office. That meant I got to deliver papers that the paperboys didn't deliver or those that got lost somehow plus whatever I was asked to do. Fortunately, this didn't last too long before I got a job at the Chicago Public Library on 104th and Ewing Avenue also on the East Side of Chicago. My job was to put back the books people returned to the library so I became well acquainted with the Dewey Decimal System used to file books in a library. Sometimes I would be dispatched to go after people who did not return books they borrowed. I was supposed to get the book and collect the fines. I vaguely recall getting some books back but I don't recall collecting much money in fines for the overdue books.

Meanwhile, my salary at the library went all the way up to minimum wage which was $1.05 per hour and I worked four hours per night, 5:00 p.m. to 9:00 p.m. every week night except Wednesdays. On Saturdays, I worked four hours from 1:00 p.m. to 5:00 p.m. for a total of 20 hours per week. This gave me a gross income of $21 per week. Then I learned about Social Security taxes. I don't remember how much they took but I know I didn't authorize it and they wouldn't let me keep my whole $21. Fortunately, I worked there through most of high school and the minimum wage went all the way up to $1.30 per hour.

Now I was making so much money, I decided to open a bank account and save my money for college. I put most of my money in the bank and kept a little each week for necessities like candy and comic books. When I finished college and got married several years later, my bank account was worth over $800. So I wasn't a millionaire yet but I was on my way.

The only problem with working four hours per night was getting my homework done. I would usually leave the library at 9 p.m. and walk home which was a distance of about one mile. Then my mom would heat up my dinner and I would eat it by myself since everybody else already ate. Then about 10 p.m., I would open my books and start my homework. I was happy when I finished it by midnight so I could get six to seven hours of sleep. Unfortunately, some nights I stayed up until 2:00 a.m. or later. A couple of times, I stayed up all night. In the morning I washed up, changed my clothes and went to school with no sleep that night. The next day was a very long day indeed. However, I think I did manage to maintain a straight A average for all four years. I think I may have gotten one B+ in my very first quarter there. After finishing high school, I got a 4 year scholarship to Purdue by doing well on a test they gave me. I also got a small scholarship from the Knights of Columbus. I think it was $100. So I guess all that hard work paid off in the end.

High School Romances

One of many memorable high school dances comes to mind. This one was supposed to be a mixer. I think it occurred during my freshman year. I think this dance must have occurred before I met Jeannine. I went with a few of my guy friends. Our gym was built around a basketball court with a stage behind one of the baskets. The boys were busy talking and holding up one of the gym walls while the girls were on the opposite side of the gym floor holding up their wall. Meanwhile someone was playing records on the stage. A few girls started dancing with each other to help them stay awake. After what seemed like forever, I told the guys I was with that I was going to ask a girl to dance. After all, what could I lose anyway. This evening was on its way to becoming one of the biggest duds in history. So when they started playing a slow song, I walked over to the girl's side of the gym and asked one of them to dance. We danced and talked for a while and before I knew it, another girl tapped her on the shoulder and asked to cut in and dance with me. My partner obliged and I resumed the dance with the new girl. Over the course of the dance several other girls cut in and danced with me. I was ecstatic. Girls actually wanted to dance with me. One girl cut in and pulled me so close to her that I thought we had to be breaking some rule by dancing so close together. I was expecting one of the teacher chaperones to tap me on the shoulder and remind me that "God was watching us." Anyway, the whole night went like that and then when it was over, I left with my guy friends. How dumb was that? Why didn't I at least ask one of the girls to leave with me? Why didn't I ask the one who liked dancing close? Maybe I could have walked her home or to the bus stop. Maybe she would have even kissed me. Who knows? I wasn't as suave and debonair as I am today since I just got out of grammar school a few months before the dance. Anyway, I had a great time and was really looking forward to the next dance on the school calendar.

One day they announced over the high school PA system that they were going to teach us how to square dance after school. It was voluntary but I had time from 3 p.m. till I started working at the library at 5 p.m. so I went. I learned that square dancing was pretty easy and so I continued going a few more times and liked it. While dancing, I met a girl name Jeannine Biegel. She was nice and she lived on 100th and Avenue M just 3 blocks south of my house on 97th and Avenue M. So she was right on my way home. So I often walked her home after school. One day on one of our walks home, she told me that some kids thought we were a good match for each other because we were both a couple of nerds. I didn't care because we were happy with each other and that was all that mattered to me. Maybe we weren't the most popular kids in school but we went to several dances, football games, basketball games, and both our Junior and Senior Proms together. We enjoyed lots of good times while we were in high school. We even went steady for a year or so. I think we decided to stop going steady when I started college. However, we still remained friends and occasionally saw each other on the East Side.

Early in our relationship there was a dance at school and I think it was the night Jeannine and I won some kind of prize that made her queen and me king for the night. (I think it was a drawing.) So we got to dance the first dance of the night. That was all. We didn't get any money or prizes or anything like that – just the first dance. I think they did take our picture together too. She had a nice dress on and I had a new sport coat to wear with my shirt and tie. I wish I knew what I did with that picture.

After the dance, I took her home and her mother was up waiting for us. She was watching some late night show on TV. I was hoping she would go to bed and leave us alone for awhile. After all, I brought Jeannine home safe and sound and we were in her living room. I stayed around and waited for her mother's TV show to end so we could have some alone time. However, when her show ended around 11 p.m., she said she liked the show that came on next and she never missed it. I had it. That was it for me. So Jeannine walked me to the front door and we kissed goodnight. That was the first time I ever kissed a girl that wasn't a relative. SMOOOOOCH. It had to be the loudest kiss on record. Her mother could have heard it from the back porch. Fortunately, we got better at kissing as we got to know each other better but that was all we ever did. We did hold hands a lot too.

For our Senior Prom, Jeannine and I double dated with my friend John Waninski and his date Anita Nommesh. John was the class valedictorian and Anita was the salutatorian. John and I wore our rented tuxedos and the girls wore fancy dresses. We stopped by my house so my parents could see what we looked like. My mom took our picture before we left. See it below. The Prom took place at McCormick Place in Chicago which was located right on Lake Michigan. When the Prom ended, we went to the Empire Room of the Palmer House Hotel in downtown Chicago for dinner. We were not yet old enough to drink. I remember having a small heart attack when I saw the bill for the four of us was $40. I thought people would have to be millionaires to afford $10 for a single meal. Fortunately, I had saved up my money for the big evening and I was able to pay the bill and even leave a tip too. While we were there, we heard Andy Williams singing in person. It was a great show and a good time was had by all. Lately I was wondering how many kids stayed home from the prom because they didn't have a date or money to go. I vaguely remember some of the kids that were there but I have no idea who didn't show up.

JUN • 62

22

AVERAGE JOE

Joe Goes Out for the Track Team

In my Junior year I decided to go out for the track team. I ran the one mile and half mile races. I wasn't very good but it was a great work out. Since our school did not have a track to run on, we would jog to Calumet Park after school. When we got there we would do calisthenics and then jog for about an hour or so. Then we would jog back to school to shower and change. Then I walked to my job at the library which was only a couple of blocks away. Then I would be on my feet working until 9 p.m. When I finished working, I would walk a mile to our house and have dinner and start my homework. During that year, my weight dropped from 180 pounds to 160 pounds in the few weeks I was on the team. Thankfully, the season was short and I was not a super athlete so they didn't need me all the time. My crowning achievement as a runner was when I came in second in the half mile run in a track meet at Calumet Park. For whatever reason, hardly anyone from school came to see us run. So the following year, I decided not to go out for the track team. I figured I had enough to do without it.

However, I did learn something by being on the track team. High school athletes have a rough life. They have to practice every day. Then on weekends or evenings they compete with other schools. As I found out, all the practice and competitions consume a major portion of their time. And all that running makes them very tired. So I figured out why most of the athletes I knew were not fantastic students. They just didn't have enough time to do all their homework assignments. Consequently, their grades suffered although I am sure their bodies were in fantastic shape when they weren't hurt. When my youngest daughter Danielle was considering playing basketball, I reminded her of this sad fact and for that reason and a variety of other reasons, she chose not to play basketball in high school. She did decide to play volleyball and was a very good player. She actually made the all-district team. She also graduated with straight As' in high school.

Fun with Biology

When I was a sophomore at SFDS, I had to take Biology. Toward the end of the year we were required to complete a big project of our own choosing. So a couple of friends and I decided to build a planter for the biology room. So we got a couple of small tables kind of like rectangular end tables. Then we made box out of wood with an open top. The sides were about 8 inches high. Then we bought some sheets of steel to put in the box as a liner. We caulked the seams so that it wouldn't leak. The planter was about 8 feet long and maybe about 2 feet wide. We filled it with dirt and planted all kinds of flowers and stuff in it. It looked great right under the windows of the biology room where the plants could get lots of natural sunlight. Our project looked wonderful and we all got A's for our good work.

Unfortunately, I found out the following year that our beautiful planter was leaking like a sieve. It seems that the steel liner was rusting away from the moisture in the dirt. I don't know if the next class fixed it or they just threw it away. But we got a good grade on it anyway.

While my friends and I were working on our project, we got to see some of the other projects the other students did. One student collected all different kinds of seeds and provided samples of each type. We got a great idea. We took some of each type of the different seeds. Then we planted them in a big flower garden outside the gym. Then we just waited to see the fun. This was the gift that kept giving all year long. Every time we went by the gym something new was blooming in the flower garden. We saw watermelon vines, tomato plants, carrots, etc. One time our poor maintenance guy was in the garden trying to remove all the unwanted plants. We could barely contain ourselves as we saw him work.

Walking home with Lillian

One Sunday morning in the summer between my high school graduation and the start of my college years, I attended mass and somehow ended up walking home with a girl from my class named Lillian.

Lillian was one of the girls I arranged to sit next to in grammar school. We had a very nice conversation. We talked about our plans after high school. I told her I was going to Purdue and was going to study Electrical Engineering and she told me her plans that I have since forgotten. She lived on the same street I did, just on the next block. So when we got to my house we said goodbye and I never spoke to her again. I often wondered what my life would have been like if I decided to call her and get to know her better. A word to the wise is appropriate here. We had a nice conversation and we could have had some more. I should have called her but didn't. If the reader finds himself or herself in the same situation, ask her if she would like you to call her. You have nothing to lose. If she's not interested, so what. At least you tried and maybe life would have been different for both of you.

Graduation Day

In May of 1962, I graduated from St. Francis de Sales High School. Along the way, I became a member of the National Honor Society and wore the cloth badge on my graduation gown. I took a test where my dad worked and my score qualified me for a four year scholarship at Purdue University. There is a picture of me and my dad at his work when I was awarded the scholarship. This article appeared in his company newsletter. Another scholarship winner named Mike Drapac became my roommate at the main campus of Purdue in West Lafayette, Indiana. We both graduated from Purdue University with bachelor's degrees in Electrical Engineering four years after this picture was taken.

Company scholarship winners were guests of Harold Hoekelman, then manager of Chicago district operations, for a luncheon and plant tour recently. Above left, seated, James Jay Cook and Hoekelman; standing, father David Cook and Frank C. McGough, general superintendent of Maintenance and Utilities. Above right, seated, father Andrew J. Drapac, Michael Drapac, and McGough; standing, E. A. Young, superintendent of Maintenance — Strip, Sheet and Tin; and Hoekelman. Below, seated, are father Joseph Brozovich, Sr., and Joseph Brozovich, Jr.; standing, Harold R. Ryan, superintendent, No. 2 Open Hearth.

Scholarship Winners Lunch, Tour Plant

By Marcia Krull
Training

The 1962 full time scholarship award winners and their fathers recently were guests of management for lunch and a plant tour. Harold Hoekelman, then manager of Chicago district and now general manager of steel operations, and other officials met with the group for lunch. The following young men received scholarship awards:

Joseph Brozovich, Jr., 9731 Avenue M, Chicago, a June graduate of St. Francis de Sales High School. His father, Joseph Brozovich, is a steel pourer in the Open Hearth Department and has 26 years of service with the company.

James Jay Cook, 6912 McCook, Hammond, a June graduate of Morton High School, Hammond. His father, David Cook, is an order planner for the Maintenance Planning and Scheduling Department and has 39 years of service with the company.

Michael Drapac, 2011 Lincoln Avenue, Whiting, a June graduate of Hammond Technical High School. His father, Andrew J. Drapac, is an electrical maintenanceman in the Tin Mill and has 32 years of service with the company.

These young men entered Purdue University Calumet Center this month. If they maintain university standards, their awards will be renewed each semester for eight semesters. The company sponsors 12 full time scholarship awards. They are available to sons of employees who qualify and whose parent has been with the company more than five years. Applications must be made through the superintendent of the department in which the parent is employed.

At some point my folks told me they were very proud of me and my academic achievements. They also told me that I was the first person in our family to graduate from high school. I had about 20 cousins on my dad's side of the family and I have no idea how many cousins on my mom's side since most of them were in Croatia. My brother John would equal my achievements four years later. Ultimately, we both graduated from college and got master's degrees. I got one and John got two. So I guess we were the only two in our family to reach that academic level until my brother John's three children earned two P.H.D.s and one law degree. John's second wife had two girls that also earned their P.H.D.s So their children and grandchildren gave the lady with a fourth grade education (mom) and the man with an eighth grade education (dad) something to celebrate.

CHAPTER 6 JOE ATTENDS PURDUE UNIVERSITY

Life at Purdue University Calumet Campus (PUCC)

In the fall of 1962, I started my college adventure at Purdue's Calumet Campus located near the intersection of 169th Street and Indianapolis Blvd., in Hammond, Indiana. It was only about 7 miles from our house and we only lived a couple of blocks from Indianapolis Blvd. I think a lot of the towns in northwest Indiana acted like small Chicago suburbs. If I had to, I could take two buses from our house to the Purdue Campus. I know that because I took them home a couple of times. Unfortunately, taking the bus took a long time and I needed that time to study.

Fortunately, our neighbor Ed Klobucar worked at the Jewel store near the Purdue campus and he volunteered to take me to school in the morning. That was a real blessing because we only had one car and my dad needed that to get to and from work. Later, after getting to know Mike Drapac, we figured out how to share our dad's cars and took each other to school. This plan worked well because Mike lived in Whiting, Indiana which was right on the way to Purdue. We were only there two years so the time flew by. When we went to the main campus, we could walk from our dorm to the Electrical Engineering building where most of our classes met.

PUCC was only a couple of buildings when I went there in the fall of 1962. I have driven by there since and it must have grown by a factor or ten or twenty. Mostly, my classes were like my high school courses except a lot harder. The students were a lot smarter too. One time I was talking to another student about high school. I thought I would impress him with the fact that I was third in my class of 130 kids. He told me he was first in his class of 800. So then I asked him what he thought of the Cubs chances of winning the pennant that year.

The one class I really enjoyed at PUCC was computer programming. I learned how to program an IBM® 1620 using the FORTRAN® (Formula Translator) programming language. I also learned how to program the IBM 1620 in Assembly language. All my programs were written on IBM cards and run on the school computer. I got an A in my class and learned that I just loved programming. Later in my professional life, I learned to program many different computers using many different languages. I even used my IBM 1620 knowledge to solve some manufacturing problems in my first engineering department at the Western Electric.

While attending PUCC, my new found friend and fellow Youngstown Scholarship winner, Mike Drapac, got me interested in cars. Mike knew how to do tune-ups and basic car repairs and he taught me how to do them. So I became the family expert on car repairs. I tuned up my car, my dad's car, my friends' cars, all for no cost. Then, once I built up my confidence with cars, I began doing repairs. I changed starters, alternators, fuel pumps, etc. I even rebuilt my own carburetor. Later I learned how to do brake jobs and other more sophisticated repairs. It became a skill I maintained my whole life and showed to my sons when they were old enough. I was even able to do some repairs when my car had problems when I was on the road away from home. Thanks to Mike for showing me all that stuff.

Joe Flunks Electronics 101

When I got to Purdue, I figured it would be like four more years of high school and basically it was. However, a lot of the other Electrical Engineering students went to vocational high schools and were already fixing radios and TVs. Some were even Ham radio operators. They knew a lot more about electricity than I did which put me at a major disadvantage in my EE (Electrical Engineering) classes. I was as good as any of them in the other classes we had to take. In the spring of my sophomore year, I took Electronics 101. The teacher was oriental and he was very difficult for me to understand. He was using a text book that was being written by a teacher on the main campus of Purdue and we were getting mimeographed copies of chapters of the book as they were being written. Unfortunately, the pages were barely legible and there were errors in them. I guess the author figured we could proof read his book while we were taking the class. So here I am in a class of about a dozen or so kids who have been playing with electrical projects in high school for up to four years and me with no experience, a teacher I can't understand, and an incomplete book with errors in it. One other kid in the class was in the same boat as me. He got a "D" and I failed the first class of life when I got my first "F".

Now what do I do? Was college really too tough for me? Should I chuck it and get a job in the mill with my dad? Heck no! I decided that I would pass that class if it kills me. I was getting A's and B's and C's in my other classes so I knew I wasn't stupid. What I needed was a plan of action.

About that time, there was a company called HEATHKIT® out of Benton Harbor, Michigan that sold electronics kits. They sold kits for TVs, radios, ham radio equipment, and lots of other stuff. They even had a catalog full of stuff you could build yourself. Since I got a job that summer working in the mill, I had enough money to buy some of those kits. I figured if I built some kits and learned how to work with them, I would gain the experience I was lacking and be equal to my classmates in hands-on experience. So I bought a kit to build a Volt-Ohm-Milliammeter (VOM). The instructions included the correct way to solder. I learned to solder and I built the VOM and learned how to use it. Then, for my next trick, I purchased an oscilloscope kit. An oscilloscope is a device that shows voltage waveforms on a small cathode ray tube display. It is very handy for troubleshooting problems in circuits. Usually, circuit diagrams show what the waveforms are supposed to look like when everything is working properly. If the oscilloscope shows a different waveform, the problem generally occurred where the actual waveform differed from the desired waveform. I enlisted the help of my friend John Waninski who was our high school class valedictorian. By some crazy coincidence he was going to the Illinois Institute of Technology to get his degree in Electrical Engineering too. So we built the oscilloscope and it worked fine. The kit also included a little box which contained small test circuits we could build and test with the oscilloscope. So that summer, we learned how to use my oscilloscope.

That summer, I also built an auto analyzer which allowed me to tune up cars. I used it to measure and adjust the dwell angle in a running engine. By the end of the summer, I could use a volt-ohm-milliammeter, an oscilloscope, an auto-analyzer and tune-up cars. My future roommate Mike Drapac was my auto-repair tutor. I never again had a problem with insufficient electronics experience. That fall, I repeated Electronics 101. My friend John Waninski. loaned me his textbook for his first Electronics course and it was infinitely better than the mimeographed papers we had. When grades came out, I just missed getting an A in EE 101 and I was on my way to my new career. The other kid in my electronics class who got the D went on to Electronics 102 (or whatever it was) and flunked it and left school never to be seen again. In the future, when I worked with new partners in lab based courses, I built the circuits and operated them and took all the measurements. I let my partners record the measurements. We were both happy with that arrangement and my experience was on a par with all the other students. If fact, I probably had more experience than most of them.

Once when we were doing an EE lab, we just couldn't get the circuit we built to work. We checked and double-checked the circuit we built and couldn't find any problems. Finally, out of desperation, we replaced the socket that held an electron tube. The circuit worked and we knew the socket was bad. We took our measurements and disassembled our circuit and left for our next class. I asked my lab partner what he did with the bad tube socket and he said he returned it to the box with all the other sockets. Nice guy huh? Hopefully, the next guy to find that bad socket would have the good sense to throw it away or give it to the teacher to fix.

Some lab classes let us do our reports at home and turn them in at the next class. One lab we took required us to finish the lab and turn in our lab report before we left. So we usually ended up with very little time to complete our lab reports and they looked it. One day they told us that they sent our lab reports to the English department to grade for English language, spelling, punctuation, etc. I barely passed the English department audit while my roommate had to go to the English department and take a remedial English class. He finally finished the class and was glad to be done with it. He went on to get a master's degree in EE, an MBA plus five U.S. patents. I assume his writing skills have improved significantly since then.

Working in the U.S. Army Corps of Engineers

I didn't work the summer after I finished high school because I knew it would be the last summer I could do that and get away with it. The summer of 1963, I worked for the U.S. Army Corps of Engineers. They were responsible for maintaining the waterways in the entire country. I worked with the group responsible for the Chicago area waterways. One of our jobs was to measure the depth of the rivers and Lake Michigan. If they got too shallow, some of the large boats would not be able to use them for fear of getting stuck in the shallow water. That would cause a major problem in the local economy because boats were used to bring coal to the mills and to ship the finished steel to their customers.

Our method of checking the river depth was very sophisticated. We had a weight on the end of a rope and little tags on the rope with the depths such as 1 ft, 2 ft., 3 ft.,… 20 feet. If we dropped the weighted line down and pulled it taught and the waterline was between the 9 and 10 foot markers, we would record the depth as 9 feet 6 inches. My job was to run another rope across the river and this rope had a maker every ten feet so the measurements would be taken at 10 foot intervals right under the markers on the rope. One guy would secure the rope to one side of the river while another guy (usually me) on the other side of the river would wind the rope around what looked like a big fishing reel. Once the line was taught, guys in a boat would make the measurements. After they took all the necessary measurements, we would move the line about 100 ft down the river and repeat the process. The readings were put on a map of the river so people could see how deep the river was at any give spot.

Problems occurred when the place I was supposed to reel up the rope was in the middle of a big weed patch with weeds 3 feet tall or taller. I had to wear coveralls to keep from getting all scratched up by poison ivy and whatever else was there. This was very uncomfortable, especially when the outside temperatures were in the 90s.

The guys I worked with were just regular guys – no college degrees. One time, they thought they had a dead car battery and so I saw this guy put a pipe wrench across the positive and negative terminals of the suspect battery. Fortunately, the battery was dead and did not explode. If he tried to do what he did to a good battery, it could have exploded and sprayed battery acid all over him and the rest of us.

Doing this job made me realize that getting that college degree might be a good alternative to spending the rest of my life working with nitwits like him.

Working in a Steel Mill

In the summer of 1963, I got a job at my dad's mill as a weigher. That's right, a weigher. I weighed stuff. I actually weighed finished steel on a big flat bed weigh scale and wrote the weight down on a piece of paper and attached it to the load of steel. One time I had to work nights from 11 p.m. to 7AM. I weighed three things all night long. That was about 5 minutes work in an 8 hour shift. My job was totally unnecessary. The guy who hooked the load of steel to the crane and unhooked it could have easily weighed the steel and wrote down the number because the crane was needed to move the steel to and from the scale. I have to confess that I fell asleep at work that night and I still got my full day's pay. Imagine that, I got paid for sleeping.

After working about six weeks, I was laid off. They needed me because they were stockpiling steel in anticipation of a strike but when the strike did not materialize, they didn't need me anymore and so they booted me out. When I got my final pay check, I saw that the mill had deducted union dues. I guess there was a rule that once you completed a certain number of hours, you were automatically admitted to the union. So I became a member of the union and dues were taken from my final check. Thanks a lot. I really needed the money because I couldn't afford the time to work while I was going to college so the money I made in the summer had to last me until the next summer. And I only worked about 6 weeks that summer. At least the steelworkers union got my pay up to $2.73 per hour before it went to zero.

Joe Becomes a Junior Engineer

The summer of 1965 was the summer before my senior year at Purdue. Youngstown, the company that gave me the scholarship hired me and my roommate Mike Drapac as junior engineers. Each week we got a new assignment so we could see how all the departments in a steel mill worked. They obviously wanted us to come and work for them after we graduated from college. I was glad to be working with Mike but I wasn't crazy about the mill. However, they did pay us $500 a month or about $250 every two weeks. $250 divided by 80 hours was $3.12 per hour. That was almost triple my original starting pay at the Chicago Public Library. So the money was good anyway.

One week I worked in the safety department. We investigated two on the job deaths. One guy got crushed between railroad cars while taking a shortcut across some railroad tracks. Another guy fell in a railroad train maintenance pit that was used so guys could work on the underside of a railroad train or car. The pit looked like a concrete grave. Did he fall? Was he pushed? We will never know. Our job was to write an accident report and that's what we did.

Another week I worked in the employment office. I gave a test to a group of potential new employees. Unfortunately, none of them spoke or read English. I guess they needed workers because they hired them anyway.

Another job I had in the employment office was to put supervisor reports into the employees' permanent records. For example, if a guy got caught sleeping on the job, he might be sent home and his supervisor would send us a note to put in his permanent record. Now the permanent record was like a big index card with the employee's name, address, phone number, etc. It had about 6 lines to report anything special about the employee. It could be good or bad. If the guy was caught sleeping, I would write that on one of the six lines for that purpose. If the guy did something good, I could enter that on one of those lines as well. However, some employee's record was so full there was no more room to write on it. There were messages on the top, the bottom, the sides, anywhere there was room on the card. I asked why they didn't fire people like this. They told me that there was a protocol when employees did something bad. For example, a first offense would result in sending them home without pay for the rest of the day. The second offense might result in the guy being sent home and a one day suspension or one day off without pay. And each offense cost the guy more money and time off from work. Finally, after some ridiculous number of offenses, the guy would be fired. However, when a supervisor caught someone doing something wrong, he had no idea what the guy's record was so the guy never got fired.

All the stuff I saw while I worked there convinced me that the steel mills were doomed. Some more efficient company would put them out of business long before I was ready to retire. So when they offered me a job after graduation, I just politely declined the job. A few years later the mills started closing. Initially customers started getting their steel from Spain because it was cheaper to ship it from Spain than it was to get it locally. Now the steel mills in Chicago and northwest Indiana are all closed as far as I know. Cars today use plastic everywhere they can instead of steel. I suppose other customers are finding substitutes for steel as well. I remember when it took a strong man to bend a steel beer can in half. Now anyone can do it because the cans are made of aluminum.

Hello MaryAnne

When we were able to drive, one of our favorite pass times was driving around and picking up girls. One day my best friend Joe Hrstich and I were riding around Whiting, Indiana which was only a couple of miles from my house. We saw two girls and stopped to talk to them. We made a date with them to go for a car ride the next day. So we picked them up in Joe Hrstich's brother's car, a 1958 Chevy Belair, and went on a ride. Joe Hrstich sat in the front with MaryAnne and I sat in the back with the other girl named Ulanda. The day was uneventful but I guess I got MaryAnne's phone number out of the deal. Joe Hrstich and Ulanda went their separate ways. I found out that MaryAnne's parents were divorced. She lived with her mom, her grandmother, her Aunt Betty and Uncle Mike. Uncle Mike was supporting that household. Uncle Mike had a good job at Standard Oil in Whiting and he never married. Uncle Mike's father passed away several years ago and he asked Mike to take care of his mother and two sisters and that's what he did for the rest of his life. He was like a father figure to MaryAnne. MaryAnne's real father was Harry Mallek. He lived on the East Side with his second wife and two kids. Soon after meeting, MaryAnne and I started dating. She was two years younger than me so she was attending George Rogers Clark High School in Whiting, Indiana when we met. MaryAnne and I went to her Junior Prom and Senior Prom together. We fixed up my friend John Waninski with her friend Theresa for at least one of the proms and the four of us had a nice time together. It didn't take too long till we were going steady. So when I went away to finish my senior year at Purdue's West Lafayette campus, MaryAnne and I were engaged. By the time my last semester at Purdue came along we were attending pre-Cana conferences to prepare us to be married.

Life at Purdue in West Lafayette Indiana

I moved to the main campus of Purdue in West Lafayette, Indiana at the beginning of my junior year in the fall of 1964. Apparently, PUCC was designed to teach us the common core stuff all engineers needed like Calculus, Chemistry, Mechanical Drawing, Physics, etc. Then when we passed all that, we went to the main campus where they had all the resources needed to pursue engineering degrees in many different disciplines, like Electrical Engineering, Mechanical Engineering, Civil Engineering, Aeronautical Engineering, Chemical Engineering, and so on.

I lived in a boy's dormitory called H4 or McCutcheon Hall. It was about a one mile walk to the Electrical Engineering building. Most days I would walk to the EE building in the morning, walk back for lunch, walk back to the EE building for afternoon classes, and then walk back to the dorm before dinner. So I walked a minimum of four miles every day just to get to and from campus from my dorm. This continued throughout my junior year. In my senior year, my parents gave me their old 1960 Dodge sedan so I could drive to school but then the problem became finding a parking place near campus.

Food in the dorm was not quite as good as prison food. The food contained lots of carbs and not much protein. For example, one day we had turkey with stuffing, mashed potatoes, corn, rolls, and cake for dessert. (It must have been Homecoming or some other big deal to get that.) The only thing with protein was the meat. When no one ate the salads, we found the lettuce from the salad in the jello the next day. I think they invented recycling at Purdue. Whatever didn't get eaten got put into the next day's jello.

While living in the dorm, my life revolved around studying, playing bridge, studying, playing chess, doing homework, and, did I mention, studying. Purdue is always one of the top ten engineering schools in the country and they make you work for every grade. I was always a B student. I got a few A's, and a few C's but mostly B's. My grades were good enough to get me into the Electrical Engineering Honorary Society which I was very proud of. One semester, I had all A's and B's on my report card. I was proud as a peacock when that happened. So I got cocky and decided to take some more challenging courses. By my last semester, I was taking mostly graduate level courses starting with the number 5, like

Math 510. That was a big mistake. I began to worry when I noticed several of my teachers were taking the same classes I was in. Apparently, they were going for their master's degrees. By the grace of God, I managed to pass all my classes that semester. Don't ask me how I did it but I know I did because I didn't get a blank diploma the day I graduated. I was really considering that possibility.

Being engaged and living 120 miles away from MaryAnne was tough. On one occasion she came down to West Lafayette to attend a dance with me. We had fun and I was planning to put her up in a hotel in Lafayette. Unfortunately, all the rooms were full so we ended it spending the night in my beautiful 1960 Dodge sedan that my parents gave me when they got a newer car. I can assure you that nothing happened that night because it was freezing cold outside. The next time she came down, I made sure she had a room before she got there.

My Near Death Experience

Purdue University is located in West Lafayette, Indiana. It is about 120 miles southeast of Chicago. In my senior year at Purdue, my parents got a new used car and gave me their old one, a 1960 Dodge Dart. Now I had a car I could use to go back and forth from my dorm to the Electrical Engineering building where I attended most of my classes. The EE building was about one mile from my dorm so the car was good to have in bad weather even though finding a parking place near campus was always a challenge. I also liked having the car because I could drive home on some weekends and visit my family and my fiancé MaryAnne. We were going to pre-Cana conferences on weekends in Whiting so we could be married as soon as I graduated.

On one of my weekend trips to Chicago, I came very close to being killed. My wonderful 1960 Dodge was a big car with a 6 cylinder engine. Pickup was measured in minutes and hours instead of seconds like most cars. When I made my trips from home to school, I took U.S. highway 41 from Chicago to Indiana highway 52 and that went right to West Lafayette. The only problem was that U.S. 41 was a four lane divided highway while highway 52 was just two lanes, one in each direction. On one of my trips going home from Purdue, I got behind a truck on highway 52. The speed limit for cars was 70 mph but I think it was considerably less than that for trucks because I can't remember any trucks ever going that fast. So there I was stuck behind this big semi waiting for a chance to pass on the two lane highway. My pokey Dodge would need at least a mile of clear road to pass that truck. Finally, I saw a big opening in the oncoming lane. So I pulled into the oncoming lane and floored it. Slowly but surely, I started to pass the semi. Inch by inch, I began to get around the semi. Then when I was about halfway by the semi, I noticed another semi coming toward me in my lane and he was closing fast. I had to make a split second decision to either drop back behind the semi or hope I could get around him before I crashed headfirst into the oncoming semi. I chose the latter. That was a big mistake. As I crept along the side of the semi, the oncoming truck kept getting closer. I finally got past his front bumper of the semi and pulled in front of him just as the oncoming semi went by me. What a relief. About a mile later, I turned onto U.S. 41, a four lane highway. That was by far the dumbest thing I ever did. I did learn from that experience however. All the cars I bought for the next several years had eight cylinder engines. I also made sure that I traveled on Interstate and divided highways as much as possible to avoid a recurrence of this incident.

Joe Gets Caught in a Blizzard on U.S. 41

When I was a senior at Purdue, I interviewed with several companies. All the companies liked me and invited me to visit the location where I would work for them. I went on three interview trips to ZENITH®, MOTOROLA® and WESTERN ELECTRIC®. Each company paid for my airfare to Chicago, rental car, meals, and hotel stay, if necessary. The trip to Motorola was the most interesting. I flew there the night before. I rented a car at O'Hare airport and spent the night at my parents' house on the East Side of Chicago. They never flew on an airplane so I guess they thought it was a big deal.

The next morning, I drove to Motorola on the northwest side of Chicago. The interview went well but they kept me late and I missed my plane back to Purdue. So I decided to drive back since I didn't want to miss any classes the next day. I stopped at my parents' house and had dinner. A big snow storm was headed our way and they begged me to spend the night. I told them I would leave ASAP and miss the storm. Unfortunately, I should have listened to them. While I was on the road, it started to snow and it got very heavy very fast. I was driving about 20 mph in a 70 mph speed zone. At this rate it was going to take me all night to go the 120 miles back to Purdue.

Then the road was amazingly clear and dry. I assumed that I reached the edge of the snow storm and I immediately increased my speed to 70mph. That was really dumb. I should have noticed that the road was plowed and not clear. Then I noticed flashing yellow lights in front of me. It was a truck moving very slowly. I didn't notice the plow on the front of the truck. So I went right by him at 70 mph. Now I was suddenly in about a foot of snow. I couldn't even tell where the road was. So I took my foot off the gas and hoped that the car would slow down before I hit anything. Suddenly, the car spun around and I was sliding backwards down the road at about 70 mph. Now what the heck am I supposed to do? Before I could think, the car did another 180 degree rotation and spun into the ditch on the right side of the road. By some miracle, I was okay but my rental car was stuck in a ditch. Now what do I do?

The guys in the snow plow pulled up to me and asked if I was okay. I told them I was fine and could they pull me out of the ditch. They said no but they could take me to a gas station that had a tow truck. So they took me there and I explained my situation to the guy there. I asked him if he could tow me out of the ditch. He said he would if I could pay him. I asked how much. He said $12. (Remember, this is 1966.) Naturally, I didn't have the money. I told him I could write him a check but he said he didn't take checks unless he knew it was good. (This was before credit cards were invented.) He said he would tow me out of the ditch if he could call my parents and make sure they would cover the check. So he called them and they said okay and reprimanded me for being stupid.

Then the guy got me out of the ditch and I drove back to Purdue at 20 – 25 mph. I think I got in around 3 or 4:00 a.m. That whole trip was awful.

When I got up the next morning, I checked the car and it didn't have a mark on it. So I took it back to the rental car company and paid them for renting it. Fortunately, there was no visible damage to the car.

Then I had to write a letter to Motorola and ask them to pay for everything including the towing. I think the whole bill for everything was around $100. They wrote back to me and told me how to write a voucher which included a hotel stay and some meals to cover all my expenses including gas and towing. So I did that and I was reimbursed for all my expenses. So I survived another miracle on U.S. 41. Praise the Lord!

Note to self: Listen to your parents. When you try to prove them wrong, the opposite usually occurs.

Graduation from Purdue University

I graduated from Purdue on Sunday, June 5, 1966 with my bachelor's degree in Electrical Engineering. My mom, dad, brother John and my friend Albert came down to see me get my degree. MaryAnne and I got married the following Saturday, June 11, 1966. The wedding ceremony took place in St. John's church in Whiting and the reception was at the Jovial Club in South Chicago at 96th and Commercial Avenue. I think we had about 100 guests. We had family style chicken, beef, mostaccioli and an open bar. I think the bill was $7 per person plus the bar. Thankfully, Uncle Mike picked up the tab because we sure didn't have that kind of money.

Chapter 7 Life after College

Married Life

After graduating from Purdue, I gave my 1960 Dodge Dart to my brother John. I bought a used Pontiac Catalina from a private party shortly before our wedding. It was a red, two door hardtop. The car had a 389 cubic inch V8 engine in it and it looked really cool. The guy sold it to me because he was going in the military. It didn't have seat belts in it but it did have the holes in the floor to hold the belts. So I bought my own seat belts and installed them myself. I probably did not use them as much as I should, but at least they were there if we chose to use them.

We drove it down to Lake of the Ozarks in central Missouri for our honeymoon. We spent a week at the Lodge of the Four Seasons. My car did not have air-conditioning so we opened the floor vents by the front seats of the car and rolled down the back windows. This gave us fresh, although hot, air flowing through the car. We had a great time. After being engaged for two years, we were both ready to be married and start a new phase of our lives.

While still at Purdue, I interviewed with Western Electric Company, the manufacturing division of the Bell System. They offered me a job at the Hawthorne Works on 22nd and Cicero Avenue in the Chicago suburb of Cicero. I accepted their offer for $690 per month. We looked at apartments in Cicero but my parents were only asking us to pay $50 per month to rent Uncle Jim's house. Furthermore, we were close to both our families if we needed them for anything.

So after returning from our honeymoon, we moved into my dad's Uncle Jim's house on 97th and Avenue N only about a block from where my parents' house was. Uncle Jim had passed away while I was at Purdue and my dad inherited his house. Oddly enough, this was the house where my father and his siblings lived when their mom could no longer care for them. When my folks married, this was the house they lived in until just before I was born.

Working at the Western Electric Hawthorne Works

I started working as an Engineer two weeks after we were married in June of 1966. I commuted from the East Side to Western Electric in the Chicago suburb of Cicero, a distance of about 20 miles. Unfortunately, my commute took me from the far southeast side of Chicago to just west of the far west side of the city, at 22nd and Cicero Avenue. My commute took about an hour in good weather and much longer when it was snowing. It sometimes took so long that I started bringing a book with me so I could read while I was sitting in traffic.

Joe and the Vietnam War

While going to Purdue, our country entered the Vietnam War and created a draft to give our military a supply of troops. College students were given a deferment while they were in college so my friends and I were exempt from the draft until we graduated. As graduation day loomed ahead of me, I decided I should do something about the draft before the government decided the issue for me. I investigated all the branches of military service to see which one would help me and my career the most. The Navy wanted me to go on a 6 month cruise in my first year. As a future newlywed, I did not find their plan workable for me. The Air Force did not want married men. That was not an option for me. The Army and Marines would take me but they had no real use for electrical engineers. So that didn't work for me either.

About that time, the recruiters on campus were talking about offering us jobs that qualified for draft deferments. Western Electric was one of those companies. They made military communications equipment and my job would have me involved in the testing of those products. That sounded good to me so I took the Western Electric offer.

When I got to work after graduating, one of my first jobs was to write a letter to my draft board requesting a deferment from the draft because I was involved in testing military communications systems. I took a letter that another engineer wrote for the same purpose and he got his deferment so I expected the letter to do the same for me. So I just changed his name to mine with a couple of other minor modifications and sent the letter to my draft board. Their reply was a resounding "No".

I showed the letter to my manager and asked what I should do. He said I could appeal their decision. So I promptly wrote a letter appealing their decision on the same grounds as before, that is, they needed and used the equipment I was responsible for testing. Of course, my appeal was denied.

Then I went to New York City to take some new-hire training courses. My wife called me in New York and told me I got a letter from my draft board. She said it ordered me to report for a physical a few days later. So I wrote them another letter telling them I was in New York and would not be able to take the physical in Chicago. My boss in Chicago offered to pay my way to Chicago so I could take the physical. I politely declined his generous offer.

Then my draft board sent me another letter telling me to report for my physical at a certain date and time in New York City. Unfortunately, I would be back in Chicago when I was due for a physical in New York. So I either called or wrote to them about my situation.

While all this was going on, Mary Anne was pregnant with our first child and she was born 271 days after we were married. She was also born before the draft board could reschedule my physical for the second time. So, when my darling daughter Joanne was born, I got a copy of her birth certificate and promptly delivered it to my draft board in person. They reluctantly gave me a daddy deferment and the matter was closed for good. They never bothered me again. Thank you Joanne and thank you God for likely saving my life.

Incidentally, I was involved in testing communications equipment for the military. I wrote the Inspection Methods Instructions (IMIs) for their equipment and I did everything in my power to insure that the equipment worked perfectly when it left our factory. So I feel like I did my part for the war effort.

My First Engineering Job

My first job was in a testset development group. A testset is used to test the products that we made and make sure that they worked before we shipped them to our customers. Since we were the only ones that needed testsets like this, they had to be designed, built, deployed and maintained by groups of engineers in departments like ours. Shop people called testers actually used the testsets to test the products that we manufactured. When they got stuck on a problem, we had to go to the shop and help them solve it so that the thing they were testing could be shipped out on time. Our customers were the phone companies. Our products were the pieces of the telephone systems that allowed people all over the world to call and talk to one another whether they were calling the people next door of their relatives in Europe.

Engineers at Bell Telephone Laboratories (Bell Labs) designed the products we made and sometimes they had to design testsets to test their own designs to make sure that they did what they were supposed to do. Sometimes, they would share their testset designs with the Western Electric Company (WECo) engineers so that all the WECo engineers had to do was duplicate the designs they got from Bell Labs. Sometimes that wasn't the best idea.

While I was working at Hawthorne, I did a lot of small projects for my department. Then one day the company decided they needed more testsets so I got the responsibility for a Signal Processor (SP) testset. The Signal Processor was a special purpose computer used by the No. 1 Electronic Switching System. The Hawthorne Works needed the testset so it could start manufacturing Signal Processors because the Columbus Works could not keep up with the demand. I got the job.

I went to Bell Labs and looked at what they used to test SPs. They invented their own test set. It was pretty old technology and used thyratron tubes as light bulbs to display errors. They were no longer available and some were already burned out. So I decided to design and build my own testset using integrated circuits. To make it more cost effective, I was going to make it a dual purpose testset and test the Central Control (CC) as well as the SP.

I decided to use integrated circuits for the test set. No one in my department had any experience with them since all the existing test sets used discrete logic circuits with transistors, resistors, etc. To make matters worse, we got a new manager who was a former magazine editor and knew nothing about electronics. He pushed me to set unrealistic dates for completing the project because he had no idea how long it would take to invent a new testset and neither did I. Then he got mad when we missed the dates. To make matters worse, he was in the habit of shouting at people in front of all the people in the building when he was mad, which was most of the time. Life was not good then. I was working 80 hour weeks and had to have the Works Manager sign my timecards.

Here is a brief description of my testset. It was basically a special purpose computer. The tester would give the testset commands from the keyboard in the front. It could also get information from the tape reader in the top left corner. Information was sent to the product under test and the test results would be displayed on the Cathode Ray Tube display shown below the tape reader. I designed everything myself including the keyboard, the CRT display, the tape reader interface, everything. The testset used over 1300 integrated circuits shown mounted vertically on the right side of the cabinet. I had to specify each part and then order it, receive it and install it, and test it and make sure it worked right.

This was a perfect situation for a minicomputer or PC but the minicomputer was not available until 1965 and the PC did not become available until 1979. Neither computer was used anywhere in the factory where I worked. I had no idea they even existed then.

While I was in the process of inventing this testset, I was still required to support the shop with their production testing. In other words, if the tester found a problem he couldn't solve, they called the engineers to help them solve it. One day I was told that a new tester was assigned to my area. He was a 38 grade fork lift operator who was promoted to 39 grade tester. This was because of the union rules. When a 39 grade job became available, the 38 grade person with the most seniority got the first chance at it. This guy was a fine man but he didn't know the difference between a transistor radio and a voltmeter. He might have been a great fork lift driver but he did not know the first thing about electronics. So I tried to train him to be a tester but it was hopeless. The union rules specified that he had to get a fair chance at doing the job. I think he got like a 30 or 60 day training period. So it took a lot of my time away from my testset to do this guy's job because he sure couldn't do it.

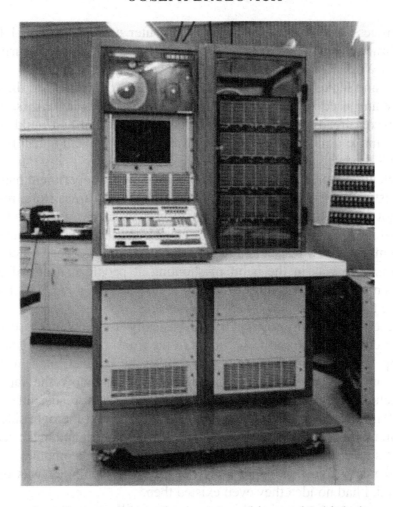

To make a long story short, I never did get the testset working and I think they sent the products they made to the Columbus Works for testing. So when one of my former managers asked me to transfer to the new manufacturing plant in Lisle, IL, I was more than delighted to go. My idiot boss asked me to document how my testset was supposed to work for my successor on the project, whoever that might be. So I spent a few weeks and created a document that ended up being over 70 typewritten pages. Every circuit in the testset was described in the document. Furthermore, I went through all the official drawings for the test set and made sure they were up to date and indicated where any changes needed to be made. Shortly after I finished the document, I was officially transferred to the Lisle Plant in 1971.

Around 10 to 20 years later, Western Electric closed the Hawthorne Plant and sold the property. I went by there after the deal was done and the new owner knocked down all the old buildings I worked in. The land became a big mall. Many of the people who worked there eventually went to work at the Lisle Plant or to other Western Electric facilities in the Lisle-Naperville area. I am guessing, but I would think that most of the shop people retired or were let go when the plant closed.

The Chicago Blizzard of 1967

In January of 1967, I was sent to an Orientation Seminar in Highland Park, Illinois. The class took place in a hotel called Moraine on the Lake. I think the place was built in the 1800s or early 1900s. Two rooms shared a common bathroom. I thought that was unusual but whenever I needed to use it, it was available and I did my business and got out of there before my neighbor needed to use it.

The place was located on Lake Michigan. One day we walked down to the lake. The weather was unbelievably nice. I think the temperature was around 65 degrees, unheard of for January in Chicago. We just walked around outside in just our shirts with no jackets.

Then the weather turned cold and it started snowing, and snowing and snowing. By the time it stopped snowing, there was about two feet of snow on the ground. I was scheduled to leave but there was no way for me to get home to the southeast side of Chicago because all the roads were closed. I never saw anything like it. All the major roads in the Chicago area like the Outer Drive also known as Lake Shore Drive, the Dan Ryan Expressway, the Stevenson Expressway, etc. looked like parking lots. The traffic got so bad that the cars were not moving. People sat in their cars until they ran out of gas. Then they left their cars where they were and walked home. I have never seen anything like it in my life.

I was scheduled to leave but no one was leaving because of the condition of the roads. I heard that the trains were running and I could use them to get home. So I left my car in the hotel parking lot, and carried my own luggage. A cab took me to the train station in Highland Park. I caught a train and took it to Union Station in downtown Chicago. Along the way, I looked out my window and saw hundreds and hundreds of cars abandoned on the Outer Drive and other expressways for several miles.

Once I got to Union Station, I had to travel to the Illinois Central Station which was several blocks away. A man in a passenger van was taking people between the two train stations. He had the only vehicle that was moving in downtown Chicago. He ran every light there was because there were no other vehicles on the streets even though the streets were plowed clean down to the pavement. I have never been downtown and seen no cars anywhere. It was like the entire downtown area was deserted.

The van took me to the Illinois Central Station where I caught a train to South Chicago. I got off the train and walked to a bus stop. After waiting several minutes, I suddenly realized that the buses might not be running because of the weather. So I started walking along the bus route toward the East Side. I figured that if a bus ever did come, I could get on it and ride it to the East Side. Unfortunately, I never saw a bus that day. So carrying my one bag of luggage, I walked the two or three miles to our home on the East Side. When I got to the residential areas, I was grateful that some people shoveled the snow off the sidewalks in front of their houses because the snow was up to my waist! The path on the sidewalks was only a couple of feet wide but at least it was better than walking in waist deep snow.

I finally got home and stayed there for a couple days until the roads were cleared so people could go to work again. When the main roads were clear, MaryAnne's Uncle Mike took me to Highland Park to retrieve my car. Unfortunately it wouldn't start when we got there. I picked up the hood and saw a blanket of snow covering the entire engine from fender to fender. So I cleaned the snow as best I could and Mike gave me jump to get started. I finally got my car started and drove it home. My life was finally back to normal again when I could drive myself to work again. The Chicago Blizzard of 1967 struck the entire Chicagoland area and northwest Indiana on January 26, 1967, with a record-setting 23 inches (58 cm) of snow falling in Chicago and its suburbs before the storm abated the next morning. To this day, it is the worst blizzard in Chicago history. Joanne was born about six weeks after the blizzard. I don't know what we would have done if she decided to make her debut during that blizzard.

Hello Joanne Marie

Here's the story of Joanne's debut in the world. Shortly after we got married, we found out that MaryAnne was pregnant. Apparently, she got pregnant on our honeymoon because our first child, a daughter we named Joanne Marie, was born nine months and one day after we were married. So I can attest to the fact that the incubation period for a human baby is indeed nine months.

The day Joanne was born, March 12, 1967, I took MaryAnne to St. Catherine's Hospital in East Chicago, Indiana. Joanne made her debut a couple of hours after we arrived which was around 9 p.m. that night. She was perfect. They brought her into MaryAnne's room and laid her in a crib right next to MaryAnne's bed. I just stared at her for hours. She had dark hair and eyes and weighed 8 pounds and 15 ounces. I just couldn't believe she was ours.

Since Joanne was born so quickly after I started working, she was not covered under my medical insurance. So I had to pay for her out of my own pocket. The total bill for everything was around $150.

It was the best $150 I ever spent.

Joanne was a great baby. She was always happy. Some days MaryAnne would leave her in her playpen for long periods of time and she would play with her feet or do whatever to entertain herself. Every time I looked at her, she had a smile on her face from ear to ear.

MaryAnne tried nursing but that didn't work so well so we started Joanne on formula. Joanne liked that just fine. MaryAnne didn't mind it either because then I could take a turn getting up at night to feed her. Since she was a pretty big baby she began sleeping through the night after about three weeks. It was great to get a whole night's sleep again.

Hello Joyce and Joseph

Since Joanne was such a great kid we decided to have another one and thirteen months later we got a big surprise. MaryAnne's doctor completely missed the fact that she was pregnant with twins. On April 5, 1968, we welcomed Joyce Ann and Joseph Paul into the family. They were both about 14 inches long and weighed slightly over five pounds each. They were also born at St. Catherine's Hospital in East Chicago, Indiana.

Joe had yellow jaundice but Joyce was fine. So we got to bring Joyce home after a couple of days but Joe had to stay in the hospital until his yellow jaundice was gone. He came home about a week later. When we went to see him in the hospital, we thought he was pretty small until we saw another baby they called "peanut" who only weighed one pound and four ounces. He was doing fine but couldn't go home until his weight exceeded five pounds. I suspect that took a while.

When Joe came home and our "little" family was finally together. So less than two years after graduating from college, I was married with three children and all of them were in diapers. Note. Disposable diapers did not come into existence until our three kids didn't need them anymore. Joanne was still sleeping the night but not so for the other two. One would cry and wake up the other one so we were very sleep deprived for the first few months after their births.

Note that the twins were born the day after Dr. Martin Luther King Junior was killed. There were lots of major riots in Chicago and all over the country when this happened. Fortunately, I didn't get caught in any of the riots. However, the incident convinced me to move to the suburbs so I wouldn't have to drive through the city every day to get to and from work. Many other people I knew did the same thing for the same reason.

Happy Holidays with our Families

After we got married, we would be invited to my family's house and MaryAnne's family's house for dinner. I think we ended up going to both houses, one for lunch and the other for dinner. That way we got to see both families and everyone was happy. After my dad passed away in 1974 and my brother got married, my mom lived alone. So we would pick her up and take her to MaryAnne's family home in Whiting, Indiana. We went there for all the holidays like Thanksgiving, Christmas, Easter, Fourth of July, etc. They would prepare huge meals for us and everyone got plenty to eat and the kids had a great time with my mom, MaryAnne's mom, Uncle Mike, Aunt Betty, and Grandma Kark.

CHAPTER 8 LIFE IN THE SUBURBS

Moving to Woodridge

After commuting from the East Side to Cicero every day, I spoke to some of my colleagues at work. Most of them lived in the far west suburbs like Naperville, Woodridge and Downers Grove, IL. MaryAnne and I went to visit some of my work friends and saw their homes and their neighborhood. We loved it there. Their home was a four bedroom, 3 bathroom raised ranch with about 2900 square feet. It also had a huge family room on the lower level and an optional two car garage. They paid about $25,000 for the house. The builder was still building them although the prices went up since my friends bought in. I was making about $12,000 per year and the home we liked cost $29,000. We were told that we could afford our house if the cost of the house was less than or equal to two and a half times my salary. Well 12,000 x 2.5 = $30,000. So we decided we could afford the house we liked and started saving for a down payment.

By the end of 1968, we had saved about $5000. We went to the builder and put a down payment down on our new home. We put $4000 down and kept $1000 for a cushion in case we needed some things we didn't know about yet. As it turned out, we ended up spending almost exactly $1000 on storm windows and screens, front and rear storm doors, gutters and downspouts and a water softener for our new home.

Since the house was brand new, we got to pick colors for all the kitchen and bathroom fixtures, tile, etc. We had fun doing it but later we wished we had chosen different colors after we saw how nice our neighbors' homes looked. The house was fine anyway and we closed on it in March of 1969. I rented a moving truck and my friends and I loaded the truck and I drove it to Woodridge where we had our new home. We started unloading the truck and carefully moving everything to the right rooms. However, by nightfall, we were too tired to do anything but empty the truck into our new garage. Over the next few weeks, we would move all the stuff to where it belonged and make room for our car in the garage.

MaryAnne and I got the master bedroom of course. Joanne got her own bedroom and the twins slept in the third upstairs bedroom. The house had three upstairs' bedrooms including the master and two other bedrooms and one more bedroom and full bathroom downstairs. The master bedroom had its own bath with a shower. There was a full bathroom in the upstairs hall. All three upstairs bedroom doors were right next to each other so we could always hear the kids if the had any problems during the night.

Lots of my coworkers from Western Electric lived in our neighborhood. A guy that started the same time I did in my department lived in the house right behind mine. We ended up being friends and ride sharing to and from the train station which became our new way to commute.

We liked the neighborhood because everyone was equal. Our homes were all comparably priced. We made about the same amount of money. We were all around the same ages and had small kids. And there were no established clicks since everyone just moved in. So we made friends with our neighbors who became lifelong buddies. MaryAnne made friends with the other stay-at-home moms. The kids made friends with the neighbors' kids and I made friends with most of my male neighbors. Some folks stayed in those houses until they died while others moved on to bigger and better houses. We stayed in the same house for about 21 years until we moved in 1990. See a picture of our first house below.

MaryAnne Was A Stay At Home Mom

While I was working in Cicero, Illinois, MaryAnne was raising our kids in Woodridge. She was a wonderful mother to our three little Indians. She joined the Mother of Twins club and became their secretary. It seemed like she was always doing something for the club.

She also volunteered to grade homework for the teachers at the St. Joan of Arc School. She not only graded papers but she got to see how our kids were doing compared to their peers. When she wasn't grading papers, she also volunteered to help with the Brownies which our girls had joined. This gave the kids more girls to play with and it helped MaryAnne find some more stay at home moms to commiserate with. After a while, MaryAnne had lots of lady friends and the kids had lots of playmates.

Woodridge was a great place to raise a family. The neighborhood was safe. The kids could play outside all day long without us worrying about them. The only requirement we had was they had to come home when the street lights came on. They usually came home without problems but if not, we could yell at them from our house and they would come trudging home.

In her spare time MaryAnne would host parties for our kids in the finished basement of our house. She would coordinate the games and dish out the cake and goodies. The kids had some very memorable birthday parties in the basement of our house. As I recall, all the kids were fairly well behaved and I don't recall having any problems with any of them although MaryAnne did most of the work. Joanne met her best friend Suzie at one of those parties and they remained friends for over 40 years.

Commuting to the Western Electric Hawthorne Works

My new commute was about a 5 to 10 minute drive to the Belmont train station in Downers Grove followed by a short train ride to the Cicero Avenue stop. Then there was about a 10 minute walk from the train station to Western Electric. The length of the train ride depended on which train I took. The fastest one went non-stop from my Belmont stop to the Cicero stop and took about 20 minutes. The other trains took longer depending on how many stops they made. I usually took the 20 minute train so I could get in early and get settled before my day got started.

The Hawthorne Works was a great place to work. I think there were about 20,000 people there when

I started. It grew so much they had to move some operations to remote buildings that were not on the main campus. They had their own railroad line which allowed them to ship and receive materials even if the truckers went on strike. The name of their railroad was the Manufacturer's Junction Railroad which was totally owned and operated by the Western Electric Company.

The Western Electric Hawthorne Works is mentioned in some Psychology courses as the place that figured out that people worked harder if you gave them more attention. So they were nice to their employees. For instance, when it was time for people to take their morning break, a huge cart with several urns of coffee plus a full assortment of pastries would show up in their work area. They could purchase what they wanted and did not have to travel to the nearest cafeteria to get it. In the afternoon, the cart appeared with cold drinks instead of coffee plus bags of potato chips, popcorn and other goodies. Naturally, everyone in my department would take advantage of all these wonderful treats whenever the cart showed up in our area. In fact, we figured out the coffee cart's path through our floor and we would hit it when it came off the elevator and right before it got on again to go to the next floor. So we got double treats. Needless to say, I gained about 20 pounds the first few months I worked there.

Once, a colleague of mine passed away of a heart attack at a fairly young age. He left a wife and a small daughter. Most companies would give the widow a life insurance check and say goodbye. Western Electric did more than that. They offered the widowed mom a job at the plant. She took the job as secretary and worked many years with the company and I am sure she was able to provide a decent life for herself and her daughter.

Joseph M Brozovich, M.S.E.E.

While I was still at Purdue one of my professors encouraged me to get my master's degree. I was pleased that he thought I was capable of doing that. So in 1967 I decided to enroll in the Illinois Institute of Technology to pursue my master's degree in Electrical Engineering. The fact that my company paid the tuition helped make that decision an easy one because I vaguely remember the cost of the courses was around $100 per credit hour. I passed all my courses with A's and B's except for one undergraduate Math class in which I got a C. Fortunately, my A's in my EE courses offset the one C and that gave me a B+ average . Unfortunately, the school required us to pass a comprehensive final to get our degrees.

Now the EE program was designed for people to get their master's degrees in one year. I took five years because I could only take one course per semester except for one time I took two. This dragged out my degree program for five years even though I took two courses at Ohio State one summer. The school had a rule that if you took longer than five years, they dropped off your oldest courses so you had to keep taking classes to get your degree. The school required us to take certain core courses for each degree program and the final exam was based on the core courses, not the elective courses that I really liked. The teachers who were currently teaching the courses made up the final exam questions. So I had to answer questions made up by teachers I never had using material from books I had never seen and the questions came from courses that I may have taken one to five years ago. Just to make it a little more challenging for us, the final was closed book although all the tests were open book when we took the courses. It took me three tries to pass that final but I finally did it in December, 1971. I noticed that the day I got my degree, one of my Purdue instructors got his P.H.D. It's a small world after all. When I got my M.S.E.E., my current manager at work got me a nice raise.

When I got the degree, I didn't think much about it, but in my later years, I realized that I was one of very few engineers who actually had a master's degree. Most of the guys I worked with just had their bachelor's degree and the associate engineers only had their Associate's degree. So I guess getting my master's degree was a pretty big accomplishment after all.

Joe the Chess Player

When I started working at the Hawthorne Works in 1966, I got a notice about a chess tournament. My friend Joe Hrstich introduced me to the game of chess when I was still in grammar school so I had been playing for a long time and considered myself a pretty decent player. So I joined the tournament. We played our games at lunch time and reported the results to the guy coordinating the event. When I called the tournament director (TD) to tell him I beat my opponent. He appeared flabbergasted. He said something like "You were not supposed to win that game". Since no one knew me, they must have figured that I was not a very good player. However, I told the TD he could call my opponent if he didn't believe me. Although I won several of my games, I did not win the tournament. However, some of the other chess players invited me to play on their team in the Chicago Industrial Chess League. This was a league that consisted of teams with players from various businesses in the Chicago area. Some of the teams were Western Electric, Bell Telephone Laboratories, Motorola, Fermi Labs, First National Bank, Sears, etc. I think there were around 30 teams in the league at that time.

There were two divisions in the league, the four man division and the eight man division. A few years later we merged the divisions into all six man teams. It has been that way ever since. The teams were divided into four geographical divisions: the Downtown division, the Near West division, the Far West division, and the North division. The teams would compete within their own divisions and the top two teams in each division went to the playoffs at the end of the year to compete for the League championship. The chess season ran from September to May. The playoffs took place in the May-June timeframe. The winning team got a trophy for their accomplishment at the annual chess banquet in June. I competed on several teams from the 1970s through the 1990s and my teams did manage to win a couple of League Championships during that time.

One nice feature about our chess league was that everyone who played got a chess rating after 5 or more games. My rating was usually in the 1700s. Over the years, we had some Chess Masters with ratings above 2200 and some experts with ratings above 2000. We also had some players with ratings around 1000. The league put out a monthly bulletin and published the ratings in the bulletin. I wrote a computer program to rate the players and show how many rating points the players gained or lost in a particular game. My program printed out all the results of the team matches, the top ten players in each division and the most improved players and how many points they gained. The output of my program generally provided over half of our bulletin content for many years. I handed off my programs and the official database of all league players to the next ratings chairman and he ported all my stuff to a personal computer the league purchased for that purpose.

Over the years I played over 200 rated games in the league and enjoyed it immensely. I met a lot of nice people and some not so nice. Generally speaking, most of the players were professional people who loved the game. Over the years, I played engineers, scientists, janitors, accountants, etc. On one occasion, one of our players beat his opponent and the opponent said he was an atomic scientist and he asked our guy what he did at Western Electric. Our guy said he was a janitor and that pretty much ended the discussion. We also learned a lot about humility playing chess.

Read all about the Chicago Industrial Chess League at http://www.chicagochessleague.org/.

Chapter 9 Joe Transfers to the Lisle Plant

Working at the Western Electric Lisle Plant

In 1971, I transferred to the Lisle Plant. AT&T® was coming out with a new line of Central Office Switches called 1A ESS® (Electronic Switching System) and No. 4 ESS. As Bell Labs was designing the new products, the charter of the Lisle Plant was to design the manufacturing facilities for those new products. Our department was responsible for designing the new testsets that would be used to test the new products. This way the products and the manufacturing testsets would be available at about the same time. Consequently, the new products could be deployed faster. Lisle was a small plant as far as manufacturing plants go so we weren't large enough to make all the new products required by AT&T. Our job was to work closely with Bell Labs to create the testsets needed for the new products. Since the Lisle Plant and Bell Labs were only about a mile apart, any problems could be quickly resolved by bringing the key people to wherever the problems were. When the products and the testsets were ready for deployment, the decision was made that the products would be made by the Oklahoma City Works. This was a huge place. They had one aisle in the plant that was a half mile long. The people who delivered mail to all the people in the plant rode bicycles. So this was exciting for me and my fellow engineers. We were like the research and development group for testsets.

Not only was my new job looking great but the Lisle Plant was only about seven miles from my new house. So my commute was reduced to about a fifteen minute drive. Furthermore, when my kids started attending St. Joan of Arc, the Catholic grammar school in Lisle, I was able to drop them off because their school was right on my way to work. Life was looking good again.

When I showed up at the Lisle Plant and met my new manager, I found him to be a very likable fellow, not at all like the magazine editor I left at Hawthorne. My new boss Chuck Richter was a test engineer at the Columbus Works and was fairly knowledgeable about testsets. We became great friends. My first assignment was to fix a Digital Equipment Corporation PDP-8® computer that was loaned to WECo by a Digital Equipment Corporation salesman. Chuck and his department were expecting to use the PDP-8 in the new test sets. Unfortunately, the PDP-8 died and no one knew how to fix it or had the time to work on it. So Chuck gave me the job.

Since I didn't have anything else to do, I gladly accepted the job of fixing the PDP-8. I got some drawings for it and the Teletypewriter™ (registered trademark of Teletype Corp) that came with it. A teletypewriter looked like a typewriter with a continuous roll of paper in it. This was how we communicated with the PDP-8 computer at that time. In a day or so, I figured out what the problem was. The problem was actually inside the teletypewriter. A relay was bad. So I asked the testset maintenance department if they could get a replacement relay and fix the problem. They did what I asked and the PDP-8 was up and running again and I gave my new boss a small sample of what I was capable of doing.

BUs Coupled Computer Aided Test System (BUCCATS)

The people at Bell Labs invented testsets to test the new products as they were being designed. Their testset worked with IBM cards. The Bell Labs engineers wrote their tests on IBM cards. Then they ran their tests and got a printout of the results. They would take their printouts back to their offices and figure out what happened. This was great for the developers of the new products. Bell Labs expected us to use their test sets in our factory.

Chuck did not like that idea. He envisioned a computer controlled testset that would be controlled by a shop tester and interactive terminal connected to a computer. The tester would run the tests from a command line interface and immediately see the test results on the terminal screen. There was no need for cards or printouts in this scenario. Chuck asked me to be the guy to write the program that took commands from the tester, sent the tests to the testset and captured the results of the tests and displayed them on the terminal.

In my previous life, I invented my own computer and human interface. This was much easier; the testset hardware was designed by the other folks in my department. The display came with the computer. So the only thing I had to do was create the computer program that orchestrated everything.

The only problem was that I never saw a PDP-8 computer in my life prior to fixing the one at Lisle. So I got some books and learned how to program the PDP-8 in Assembly Language. The PDP-8 was a 12 bit computer, vastly inferior to the 64 bit computers we use today. I think it had like 8 instructions. However, by the grace of God I learned how to program it. The engineering responsible for the testset hardware told me what I had to do to communicate with the testsets. The testset engineers invented an interface for a CRT (Cathode Ray Tube) display and provided me with instructions for communicating with the keyboard and display.

After a few months, I had my program working. The shop testers could run the tests, single step through the tests, loop over a selected group of tests, insert breakpoints where they wanted the tests to stop, and more. Furthermore, since all the testsets looked the same to the computer, my program could be used to control all the different testsets. However, each testset had to have its own computer to control it.

Needless to say, things were finally going well at work. My program worked and worked well. If any of the other engineers requested a change to my computer program, I could give them whatever they asked for very quickly since I became the in-house expert on the PDP-8 computer. The test system became known as the BUs Coupled Computer Aided Test System (BUCCATS).

MTS11 - Modular Test System Using the PDP-11® Computer

The BUCCATS testsets worked well but they were difficult to construct and debug. The testset circuitry was contained on several big panels perhaps one foot by two feet in size. Each panel probably held hundreds of integrated circuits. Whenever there was a problem with a testset, an engineer was required to solve it because of its complexity. So a decision was made to create new hardware that would be easy to build and maintain.

About this time, a new engineer named Tom Melton came to the Lisle Plant. He had the responsibility of making my first testset work so he had lots of questions for me. We became great friends and we also became co-workers when it was decided that my old testset was no longer needed. Tom and I began the design of new hardware for a modular test system. Instead of individual integrated circuits being plugged into huge panels, we got the idea of creating a family of special purpose circuit boards about the size of a human hand. We designed circuit boards that would send signals to the product under test called driver boards. We could put 32 driver circuits on a single board. Then we did the same for receiver boards which captured the response from the product being tested. Then another engineer named Ed Bluma designed a timing board which orchestrated the timing between the drivers and receivers so that the signals were sent and received in a synchronized fashion. So the computer would load the driver boards with data to be sent to the product being tested. The timing board would tell the driver board when to send the data. The data would be sent and the receiver boards would be told when to capture the response from the product being tested. The reply would be compared to the expected reply in the computer. If the reply matched, the test passed. If not, the testset would stop, display the error and await troubleshooting instructions from the tester.

The system worked great. Each driver board was connected to one and only one cable connecting it to the product being tested. It was the same for the receiver boards. So when the response from the product was incorrect and the product was working properly, the testset had to be at fault. So a tester could trace the cable back to a defective circuit board inside the testset. Then he could tell the testset maintenance person to replace a particular driver or receiver board in the testset and never have need for an engineer. Or, if the tester and the testset maintenance guys had no idea what was wrong, they could replace the circuit boards one by one until the problem was solved. Then the testset maintenance person could take the defective board back to their repair shop to troubleshoot and fix the defective circuit package. We provided a test program for them to use for that purpose. I wrote the PDP-11 program that communicated with the testset and the tester.

In 1974, two colleagues and I wrote an article about MTS11 in the Western Electric Engineer, an internal company magazine. Our project worked and worked well. The system was successfully deployed at the Oklahoma City (OKC) Works and I never got any complaints about anything not working properly, hardware or software. In fact, I never met the engineers from OKC. I went to OKC at some point in the future and took a tour of the plant. I was pleased to see that several of our testsets were deployed and in use at OKC. For the record, that PDP-11 computer with a 1.2 megabyte disk drive and operator terminal cost approximately $25,000 in 1970s dollars.

Replacing a Paper Tape Reader with a Computer

One day my friend Tom Melton and I were sitting at our desks minding our own business when our boss came in to ask us if we could replace an 8 channel paper tape reader with a computer. He said they were testing a particular product with a big reel to reel tape reader and they were unhappy that they had to wait several minutes for the tape to rewind to test the next product. We said we could do it. Tom wrote the program to generate the codes that came from the tape reader and I interfaced the PDP-11 computer to the testset.

One problem our manager anticipated was that the testset operators would need computer training and would expect a promotion now that their job would require them to know how to use a computer in addition to everything else. To avoid this problem, I added two buttons to the testset control panel, START and CONTINUE. The two new buttons basically replaced a similar two buttons the operators used to control the tape reader. The testers were instructed to press START to begin the test and CONTINUE to resume the test after an error stop. The two buttons were connected to the computer through my interface. At no time were the testers required to touch the computer or have any interaction with it. Tom loaded his computer program onto the PDP-11 and we took it to the shop. We tested the two buttons and they worked fine. Our manager was delighted that we saved the shop a ton of time with our invention. I'll bet the project took us less than a week to implement. It was probably a huge cost reduction, since all the tape rewind time was eliminated. However, we never did the paperwork to collect any savings. We did get to see our invention work and work well. The shop liked it and the testers could use it from day one with no additional special training or computer knowledge.

Sharing a Line Printer with Two Different Computers

One day our manager told us the shop needed our $12,000 line printer and they were going to take it away from us and use it with the 1A Processor computer in a System Test environment. Tom and I were not too happy about giving up our line printer that we used every day. So I decided to create an interface that would allow us to share our printer with the other computer. So I designed and built the sharing circuit and mounted it on a board inside the PDP-11 computer. It worked fine and both computers had access to the line printer whenever either needed it. If both computers tried to use it at the same time, it would look busy to the computer that lost the race to access it. Of course, I designed it so our computer would always win if there was a conflict. This little project only took a couple of weeks and we got to keep our line printer.

CHAPTER 10 LIFE IN THE 1970S AND 1980S

Joe and the Voice Storage System

Around 1977 my manager at the Lisle Plant told me he had to reduce the number of people in his department. He offered to give some of his poor performers to other groups that had job openings but the other groups didn't want poor performers; they wanted the top performers. My manager told me that if I didn't transfer to another organization that he would have to lay off a good friend of mine. So I left the Lisle Plant and went to work at the Bell Labs Indian Hill location to create a test system for the new Voice Storage System.

At that time, Bell Labs was in the process of inventing a system that would replace all the answering machines with one central voice storage system (VSS) controlled by the phone company. They envisioned this feature as a new revenue source for the company. The new VSS would be a satellite office that could connect to multiple telephone office simultaneously and store and retrieve voice messages for all of them. They needed a test system that would simulate the telephone offices requesting voice storage services.

They had already designed and built the hardware but they needed a computer to control it. Before I got there, they already picked the Digital Equipment Corporation DEC PDP-11 computer. That was exactly what we used in the factory for the MTS11 project. However, they wanted to run their own in-house operating system called MERT (Multi Environment Real Time) operating system. I suggested doing it the way we did it in the factory with the DEC operating system but they said no and I had to do it their way.

So I led a team of four people Joe, Warren, Duane and myself. We got everything working in a few months. A phone was connected to out testset hardware just like it would be to a real telephone office. We did this because the changes were not completed yet on the real telephone system.

A person would call the number, let it ring a few times and then a voice would come online and play either a personal message or a canned message like "The party you called is not available; at the tone please leave your message". The caller would leave their message and the test system would send it to VSS to store. Then when the called person came home, he would hear a stuttered dial tone and know he got a message. He would dial a special code like *57 and the system would tell him "You have 1 new message. Press *56 to get your message". So when he did that, we would ask VSS to send the stored message to the caller. It took awhile, but we finally got everything to work. Our department head made an appointment with all the vice presidents of AT&T to demonstrate the new system at AT&T headquarters in New Jersey. Note that people his level were serving coffee to the VPs at this meeting so he was pretty nervous about doing this so he told us to not change or even touch anything until after the demo. He practiced leaving a message and retrieving a message for weeks before the big demo and finally, the big day came.

I was in my office with a couple of colleagues enjoying my morning coffee when my manager came into my office and told us the demo was scheduled to start in half an hour and it doesn't work. Our department head was frantic in New Jersey. He had tried it dozens of times and it just didn't work. So I went to the lab where our test system lived. I looked at a printout of all the transactions for that morning. I noticed that when he was supposed to enter a code like *56, our system heard *55 instead. So I told my manager to tell him to enter the correct code. He informed me in no uncertain terms that he did enter the correct code. There were twenty minutes to go before the demo. It occurred to me that when he pressed the 5 key, somehow the 5 went away and came back as another 5 so we heard *55 instead of *57. Now there were 15 minutes to go before the demo. So I asked if any of our commands used the same number twice. They told me no. So I modified the control program to throw away the second number if it duplicated the first number. Now there were 10 minutes to go before the demo. I entered the program fix in the computer and quickly tested it. It worked ok. Zero time left. The demo was starting NOW. We had a big speaker in the ceiling of our lab so we could hear what was being said on the phone. Our entire department, about 50 people, were now in the lab watching (actually listening to) the demo live from New Jersey.

Our Department Head called the lab. The phone answered and said "The party you called is not available; at the tone please leave your message".

Then he said:"th th th this iiis JJJ JJJ JJJ John Smmmith, pleeeeease caaaaall meeee on 555-1212". He was so nervous he could hardly talk. Then he hung up.

He called back and retrieved his message and the demo went perfect except for his nervous message. We all let out a big cheer and celebrated with a nice long lunch at the local pub.

Joe Installs an In-ground Pool in his Backyard

In the summer of 1976, my friend Tom Melton told me how he and his brother Greg installed an in-ground pool in the backyard of Greg's house in Westmont. This got me thinking and so I asked Tom if he thought we could put an in ground pool in my backyard. Of course, he said yes. I told MaryAnne about it and she obviously liked the idea. I told her if we did it that we would be spending the rest of our summer vacations in our back yard and she agreed. So we looked for our new pool in various stores in our area and finally found the one we liked. It was a rectangular pool 16 feet wide and 32 feet long. It was 3 feet deep on the shallow end and 8 feet deep on the deep end. It came with a skimmer to suck the leaves and bugs off the surface of the water. It also came with a main drain in the bottom of the 8 foot section. The skimmer and the main drain went to the pump which sucked the dirty water from the surface and the bottom of the pool, filtered it, and then sent it back to the shallow end of the pool. When it was very hot out, the deep part of the pool had the cold water. So the main drain took the cold water and the pump returned it to the shallow end where it quickly warmed up. The pool cost around $3000 and included the digging of the hole for the pool. It even came with a book showing people how to do it. The salesman told us some 90+ year old woman installed it by herself. Yeah right. This guy is now selling snow to people who live around the North Pole.

So we bought it. They dug the hole and left the pool stuff in my garage. I saw all that stuff and said what the blank am I going to do now?

First I had to have a guy with a truck come out and take away the dirt that the hole digger left in my yard. Then I bought a case of beer and asked my friend Tom to help me install the pool. The hole for the pool had a ramp that connected the shallow end to the deep end. It also had a shelf indented in the dirt at the same level as the shallow side so we could mount the sides of the pool in a track on the shelf around the pool. The sides of the pool were Styrofoam panels that fit into an aluminum track that sat on the shelf around the pool. So before we poured the concrete, we had the panels setup all around the sides of the pool. Then we installed the pipes for the water lines from the skimmer to the filter and from the main drain to the skimmer. Lastly we put the forms in the bottom of the pool for the concrete that would go all around the main drain.

Next came the cement truck. The cement truck policy is to give you around 5 minutes per cubic yard to get the concrete out of the truck. He poured the pad for the cabana but he couldn't get the concrete to flow all the way to the far end of the pool so we had to wheel it in wheelbarrows. And we had to do it fast. The clock was running. Have you ever picked up a wheelbarrow full of concrete? It must weigh hundreds of pounds. When I tried to pick it up the first time, I thought I pulled both of my arms out of their sockets. Then just to make it easier for us, the cement truck driver filled the wheelbarrows to the brim. Nice. Real nice. Thank you for that. I think we had two wheelbarrows so Tom and I could both wheel the concrete from the truck to the pool. Boy were we smart or what? I wish I had the number for the 90 year old woman who did it herself. I was just wondering how she managed the wheelbarrow full of concrete.

So we poured concrete for the main drain. Then we poured concrete in the shelf where the sides were inserted into the track. So we ended up with the pool incased in a ring of concrete just like the instruction book said. They should have said to have an ambulance handy when doing this. Here we are. We were two normal guys who work at a desk all day, wheeling concrete around my back yard. We are lucky we didn't kill ourselves. Fortunately, no one died that day and we celebrated our victory with several tall cool beers. Before locking the sides in with concrete, we put a track on top of the panels to hold the top of the panels together. Before dropping the liner into the pool, we dumped a load of sand into the pool and spread it around with shovels so it would be nice and soft for swimmers to walk on. We also filled the shelf with sand all around the pool all the way to the top of the panel but left room for more concrete so we could pour a concrete pad all around the pool.

A few days later, the cement truck came again. This time we poured the top layer of concrete so we filled the gap between the edge of the pool and the patio with concrete. We put concrete all the way around the pool so there was a walkway for swimmers.

After pouring the concrete, we inserted the vinyl liner into the track and let the liner drop into the pool. We cut the holes for the main drain and the skimmer and the two holes in the shallow side where the clean water from the filter came into the pool.

We hooked up the filter to the electrical outlet on the patio, filled the pool with water and prayed. With the help of my neighbor's garden hose plus my own, we filled the pool in about two days. It took 18,000 gallons of water.

We put up a make shift fence to keep interlopers out and invited the kids to swim in our new pool. The water was cold as ice but they didn't care. They were the only kids in the neighborhood who had an in-ground pool. They were swimming in our pool one week after they dug the hole. I think that was the biggest accomplishment of my life.

There's more regarding building a real fence and cabana but I'll skip that part for now. Needless to say the pool was a big hit with the family and their friends. All the kids learned how to swim and they had fun diving off our board. See picture of pool below:

Later in life, I found out that a pool membership is a whole lot cheaper than installing and maintaining your own in-ground pool. Expenses incurred by me for my pool in addition to the initial cost included at least two or three extra liners at about $500 each, hundreds of dollars worth of chlorine and other chemicals each year, water for the pool, and electricity for running the filter almost 24x7 for the entire summer.

There was at least one additional expense. My pool developed a leak in the water line running from the skimmer to the filter. Remember these water lines are under concrete. So I had to rent a jackhammer to bust up the concrete to replace the broken water line. Then I bought some wood decking to go where the concrete was removed. This was by far, the worst investment of time and money in my entire life. Furthermore, the pool also presented some real problems when trying to sell the house fourteen years later. I had to put up a sign saying I would remove the pool at my expense in order to sell the house.

Amy Joins the Brozovich Family

In March of 1977 we were pregnant again. MaryAnne called me at work and said that it was time to go to the hospital. So I came home and took her to Edwards Hospital in Naperville, Illinois around noon. We got there and the nurses checked her and said she would be awhile. I should have gotten suspicious when her doctors remained in their office seeing patients while she was in labor at the hospital. I stayed with MaryAnne all day long and Amy never came. About 8 p.m., her doctor showed up and said they would have to do an emergency C-section to get Amy out. I agreed and they took MaryAnne to have her C-section.

Sometime later, the doctor found me and told me MaryAnne was fine and so was Amy. He told me MaryAnne was in the recovery room and would be out soon. Then a strange thing happened. A voice came over the PA system and said "Dr. L wanted in the recovery room." I figured something must be wrong with MaryAnne or Amy because he had been with her alone for the last several hours. I prayed that everybody was okay. The doctor finally returned a little later and told me that MaryAnne woke up and removed the breathing tube that they put in her throat to help her breath and the nurses were having difficulty getting it back in. The doctor replaced the breathing tube and all was well. Later they let me see MaryAnne and she was fine and Amy was fine too. Thank God. I finally got home around 4 a.m. Fortunately, everything went well and we brought Amy home a few days later.

Doing Projects around the House

After moving into my new house, I decided that I was going to make some changes. The first thing I did was to divide a big unfinished room in the basement into two smaller rooms. One was a laundry room and the other was to be my den.

I built a wall with a door to divide the unfinished area. Since the circuit breaker box was in the laundry room it was easy for me to add a circuit to give me a bunch of electrical outlets in my new den. I made a workbench all along one wall with a pegboard on the wall above it to hold all my small tools. I put in a drop ceiling and tile on the floor. My den was complete. Then I bought an old used metal desk and got a free sofa some neighbors were throwing away. I then added two old oak file cabinets I got for one dollar each. Now I had my man cave. I kept my power tools in there as well as other things I considered too dangerous for my kids touch. I also installed a lock for my door but I don't think I ever locked it. My kids knew my boundaries and they respected them.

My friend Tom Melton was a huge help to me in all my projects. With his help, I installed an in-ground pool in my back yard, a shed to hold the pool equipment and toys, a wooden fence around the pool, concrete walkway around the pool, a central air-conditioner for the house, a real brick fireplace in the family room, a new water heater and a new back porch. I also put drywall in my garage and created a storage space above the cars in the attic of the garage. I also made a picnic table in 1976 that is still in use at my son's house forty years later. I also made several bookcases that survived to this day.

Joe Gets His First Home Computer in 1979

In 1979, the first personal computer was available and cheap enough for home users. So I bought my very own Apple II+® computer. It came with some games and other productivity software. Initially I got the computer and one floppy disk drive. Later I added a second floppy, a monitor and a printer. When all was said and done, I had invested over $3000 in my home computer system. I imagine that $3000 would be more like $10,000 in today's money. Everybody in the family wanted to use it. MaryAnne used it to make address labels for some real estate person who paid her for the labels. The kids liked it for the games. I used the word processor for creating tests for some classes I was teaching at the time.

My son Joe was the hit of the neighborhood because we were only one of two families in our neighborhood who actually owned a home computer. Joe's friends came over often to play all the new computer games. The Apple II+ was a great new toy for everybody in our house.

My son Joe found the best use for it when he was in seventh grade. He used it for his school science fair project. His project was to determine the best brand of paper towels. He thought up a whole bunch of experiments he could do with them. In one experiment, he wet the paper towels with water, spread then over a coffee can and dropped pennies on them until they broke the through the towel. He repeated this experiment several times for best results. What was amazing about his project was the fact that he graphed all his results using a computer program. He was the only student who had computer generated graphs. He took the graphs he created and mounted then on some old pieces of paneling I had and made a great display. Then he typed up his results using the computer and had that available for the judges. Needless to say, he got an A+ on his science fair project and impressed everybody with his computer know-how. He went on to graduate from college with a degree in computer science and today he runs his own computer consulting company. I guess that computer was a pretty good investment after all.

Shortly after getting our home computer, Joyce was having a problem in school learning all the United States and capitals. So I wrote a program for our computer which would ask for all the capitals of the states. If Joyce got the correct answer, she would not see that question again. If she missed it, the program would give her the correct answer and randomly ask the question again. So she worked and worked on the program till she got them all right. Then she took the test in school and got a perfect score. Her teacher was proud of her because she even spelled all the answers correctly. I saw that the program could be easily modified to ask any questions so I changed it and gave it to her teacher with instructions on how to add her own questions. I came back some time later and saw they were still using my program. I guess it worked well.

One day when my son Joe was still going to grammar school, his teacher told the students to make a list of all things they did with their fathers. Joe said he filled one sheet of paper with stuff and was still writing when the teacher finally had to take his paper from him. He said some kids only had a couple of things on their papers. He seemed to be pretty fond of the fact that he had more things to do with his dad than any other papers he saw in class that day. I was surprised too.

Michael John Joins the Brozovich Family in 1980

When MaryAnne was pregnant with my second son, Michael, I took part of the family room and made it into a bedroom for Joanne and Joyce. I saved up all my vacation till the end of the year so I could take off all the time from Thanksgiving to New Year's Day. I took part of our family room and made it a big bedroom for the older girls. I used that time to build a wall, a doorway, a wooden floor, two closets, and added new carpeting and ran electric lights into the new bedroom. I painted it and put one bookcase for each girl in their new bedroom. I completed it before I ran out of vacation days. Then the girls moved into their new room and when Michael arrived, he got one of the upstairs bedrooms next to the master bedroom.

Michael was born in Central Dupage Hospital in Winfield, Illinois on the day after Thanksgiving in 1980. He was a planned C-section. There was way less drama for Mike than what we got with Amy. I was in the delivery room when he was born. The doctor made an incision in MaryAnne's abdomen and picked up Michael and handed him to the baby doctor in the delivery room. That only took about five minutes. Then the doctors spent the next hour sewing up all the layers of skin they had to cut through to get to Michael. Fortunately for me, they had a curtain up by MaryAnne's naval so I couldn't see all the stuff they were doing. Without that curtain, they might have needed another doctor for me. I was talking to MaryAnne and telling her what a great job she did with Michael. Michael is my middle name and MaryAnne's Uncle's first name. Uncle Mike's middle name was John so we made our Michael's middle name John as well. Michael was a large baby (around ten pounds) and healthy. MaryAnne came through the ordeal just fine. The doctors told me Michael would be a big boy and they were right on with that prediction. A few days later I took MaryAnne and Michael home to meet his siblings.

Young Joe Becomes an Auto Mechanic

When I started doing work on my cars, my son Joe was eager to help. At first he was my gopher. When I was working on something under my car, I would ask my son Joe to fetch various tools for me. He was glad to it and it made the tasks a lot easier for me. One day he and I replaced a water pump on one of my cars. A few years later, he wanted to borrow my car to go to a dance at school. I told him no because the water pump was leaking and I did not have a chance to fix it. The pump only cost $15 but it was over $100 to install it. I took it in to a couple of places and they said they couldn't get to it for at least a week. So Joe volunteered to replace my water pump. I said okay but I wasn't sure he was capable of doing it. He took me to work that morning. At 5 p.m., he picked me up at work in my car. I asked him if he was able to replace the pump. He said yes. I looked under the hood and sure enough there was my brand new water pump. He took his girlfriend to the dance that night and we never had another water pump problem with that car. And my son saved me the $100 it would have cost me if I had to pay for the work.

Another time, I went to a store to buy something and I couldn't get the car started. We tried jumping it but it still wouldn't start. So I took my other car to the auto parts store and got a new starter. Unfortunately, the way the parking lot sloped, I couldn't fit under the car to replace the starter. I asked Joe to do it. He got under the car and I started handing him the tools he needed. In about 30 minutes, he had the new starter installed. I started the car and we drove it home.

In 1985, My "Come to Jesus" Talk with Daughter Joanne

While a senior at Downers Grove North High School, my oldest daughter Joanne was planning to go to college. While attending high school, she explored her creative side taking classes like art, photography, drawing pictures, making things out of ceramic material, etc. She got fairly good grades but the classes were not really preparing her for college. So when she told me she was planning to go to Illinois Benedictine College, I felt the need to have a serious talk with her about school. I told her that tuition at IBC would cost us about $3000 per semester. I told her that was a lot of money and if she decided to go there, she had to change her ways. I told her that I wanted to see her take all mission critical courses. I also told her that she was on a one semester renewable scholarship. If she got good grades (B or better) in all her classes, I would renew her scholarship for the next semester. If she didn't meet my requirements, her scholarship would be terminated and she could go work at KMART® for the rest of her life because she was working there part-time while attending high school. Apparently, she heard my message and she managed to get a B+ average throughout all four years of college. In June of 1989 she graduated with a bachelor's degree in International Business and Economics with a second major in Spanish. Today we laugh about my little talk with her but she knew I meant business and she became a great student and never had problems in school again.

In 1988, A Company Physical Changes Joe's Life Forever

While I was working there, Western Electric provided its employees with a free physical examination every five years starting at age 40. So sometime after turning 40, I had my exam. I had to answer a bunch of health questions as part of the exam. Fortunately, the only thing I had to answer affirmatively was that I had some allergies and I was somewhat color-blind. As I got older, I had to answer more and more of those questions affirmatively.

The final part of the exam was a talk with the doctor. He gave me the bad news. I was overweight. My cholesterol level was around 300. I was in sorry shape for a 40+ year old man. I asked him if exercise would help. He said yes but take it slow because I wasn't 21 anymore. He also told me that how long I lived wasn't as important as how well I lived. Did I want to be a healthy senior or sitting in a wheelchair with my oxygen mask when I hit retirement age? I asked if I was well enough to start exercising. He said yes but take it easy.

I found out that Illinois Benedictine College had an executive fitness class in the mornings three times a week. So I joined up and got up at 5 a.m. and went to my first session a couple days later. I saw that most of the guys there were way older than me and they were all doing the exercises together. So I just joined right in. First we do some stretching and that was no problem. Then we started doing light exercises like 20 jumping jacks and I did them. Then we did 20 pushups but I couldn't do all of them. And it continued this way for like 30 – 45 minutes. Then we were supposed to go jogging. I went to the locker room and laid on the bench. People asked me if I was okay. I lied and said yes. I was exhausted and it was only 6 AM.

I told the instructor what I did and he told me not to try to keep up with the other folks in the class. They were older than me but they were in shape and I wasn't. So when they did 20 of something, I did 8. Gradually, I started doing more and more until I could do everything the other folks did. After exercising, we all went jogging. In the beginning, I ran a few laps in the gym and then showered and went home. As I got healthier, I started jogging. I eventually got to where I got up early and jogged three miles every other day.

When I was working at the Hickory Ridge Conference Center, the fitness center offered a class to help people lose weight. So I took the class. In six weeks, I dropped 25 pounds. I felt great, looked good, and had to buy some new clothes because all my old clothes were now too big for me. My life changed forever. Since then I have always continued to exercise regularly. Along the way, I had my body fat analyzed. They told me I had 17% body fat which was excellent for a guy my age.

When I went to my 50th high school reunion a few years ago, I was one of the few people without any hair-raising stories about health problems. Several of my old classmates had heart attacks. One guy even had a heart attack while he was driving down a busy street. One of my high school chums had a liver transplant. Some people were way overweight. I thought I faired better than most and not as good as others. However, I was happy that I took that doctor's advice and started my regular exercise regime. My dad passed away of a heart attack when he was only 60 years old. I am 72 years old and have few heath issues but I do take some prescription drugs to handle the problems exercise can't fix.

After retiring at age 54, I continued to get annual physicals. I also read the book "The 8 week Cholesterol Cure" and started taking time-release niacin to lower my cholesterol. I got it down to about 200. I still take the time-release niacin for my cholesterol but I had to lower the dosage because my cholesterol started to approach 100, which I was told is too low. I was happy to see that I can make my cholesterol numbers anything I want by adjusting the amount of niacin I take. Furthermore, I had no side-effects from the time release niacin, although I did get muscle cramps from the regular niacin.

Playing with Mike and Amy

In the middle 1980s, when Mike and Amy were old enough to run around by themselves, I often took them to Pioneer Park in Downers Grove to play. The park had monkey bars and slides and we could fish in the pond there. Sometimes we fished and caught a few little fish but nothing big. I also took them for walks around the pond which was at least a half mile walk, if not more. When we finished our little excursion at the park, I took them for ice cream. I think that was their favorite activity. Guess what, they slept like logs when we got home. Mission accomplished.

I never gave much thought to taking the kids to play in the park. However, it did make quite an impression on my daughter Amy. She wrote me the following letter for my 70th birthday.

Dear Dad,

Thank you for giving me the opportunity to share some of my special memories with you. As your favorite daughter, (insert smirk) I have many memories and will start with some of the earlier ones.

Do you remember walking around the lake at 55th Street Park? I remember looking for frogs, jumping fish, and running from Michael. When fishing there, we occasionally caught a blue gill, some sunfish and bull heads. I also remember working up to crossing the monkey bars on my own there. My success was celebrated with a DQ cherry dipped ice cream cone. I loved spending those evening hours with my daddy.

In fact, I have many fond memories of fishing with you. And I love that I've been able to make some special memories with my own kids while fishing. From catching and releasing in local ponds, to catching and keeping while we were in WI. We would head out on the lake, at 'ramming speed' and then slowly creep up the fishing hole, where everyone else was. The year we took Pudgy, I'm not sure we caught many fish. The terrier in her took over and scared all the fish from the lake when she went bonkers over a disappearing bobber...boy she knew what was coming! We loved that dog and spending time with her.

As time went on, I remember spending "long" drives with you out to Grandma's house, usually with a bag in tow, so I could stay for the week. I enjoyed having you all to myself so I could share stories about what was going on in my life. Just as well, I enjoyed listening to how those stories related to the stories you told me about when you were a kid. We talked about what it was like growing up in the city. Like having a paper route, being an altar boy, and working hard in school. Though so much time had passed since you were a kid, so much remained the same in life in general.

As I got a little older, I remember fitting in and going out with my friends. Dressing appropriately for my body type was not always easy, when most of my friends were smaller than I. It seemed they could get away with much less. But I remember you telling me "Most girls would die to look as good as you." And even if the words did not seem like much, they really helped my self-esteem. Besides, most days it really didn't matter what others thought of me, it was you I most wanted to please anyway.

That is also how I remember college too. As terrible as my first quarter at COD was, you never gave up on me. Telling me I could be whatever I wanted to be as long as I worked hard. You encouraged me, telling me I would be great at whatever I was going to do. And you're right Dad I am great at what I do. Every employer I have had appreciates me and what I have to offer. I enjoy being a go-to person and helping others problem solve. I enjoy working with and training others. The truth is though, that's not what I learned at school, but what I witnessed at home. The hard-working dad that I looked up to could do it all. You were (and still are) a superhero!

Looking back though, most of my favorite memories revolve around the holidays. I love that the most important holidays start with mass. Whether at St. Joan, St. George, St. John, or St. Margaret Mary, the most important days of the year started in the house of God. Christmas and Easter were full of gifts and sweets, family, and food. But, I know now that the most important gift you ever gave me dad, was my faith. I thank you so much for the sacrifices you made so that I could attend a Catholic school and be raised along-side so many special families. In fact, until I went to high school, I thought everyone was Catholic. Why wouldn't they be? I had peace, knowing that God the Father loved me more than even you and mom. This especially came in handy during high school and my most difficult growing years.

I was so lucky to have a role model at home who taught me the differences between right and wrong...the one who answered when his mother called and helped his neighbors in need. It was you dad, who was planting the seed of unconditional love. It was you living your life the way we should live ours. It was you who helped to establish this family of faith and love. You, who taught us how to be a parent. I hope I am just as good to my kids as you were to us.

Thank you for continuing to walk with us in our journeys as adults. No matter how big I get, I still enjoy bopping around the pool and chatting with you on noodles. I love to share the first cup of coffee around the Sunday morning paper. It reminds me of butter and jelly sandwiches over the Sunday Tribune. I remember browsing the funnies while you checked out the front page. Then, after church, we'd retreat to the couch to watch wrestling while you folded laundry. I also enjoyed curling up to watch Saturday morning cartoons on the velour, flowery couch.

There are so many more, but these are certainly a few of my favorite. I thank you dad for all the great memories we've made so far and I look forward to creating even more.

Happy Birthday Dad...

All my love,

Amy

Amy Repairs Grandma's Vacuum

On one occasion I took Amy to spend a week at my mother's house in Chicago. While she was there, my mom went to vacuum the house and the vacuum stopped working. Grandma didn't know what to do but Amy did. She turned the vacuum upside down and took the plate off the bottom. This revealed a broken belt connecting the motor to the beater bar. So she and grandma took the broken belt to the local hardware store on a city bus. They asked for a new belt just like the one they brought in. The friendly hardware man sold them the belt they needed. When they went home Amy replaced the belt in the vacuum and Grandma finished vacuuming her house. Grandma often bragged to her friends about the day her 10 year old grand-daughter fixed her vacuum. When grandma asked her how she knew what to do, she proudly said "I watched my dad do it".

CHAPTER 11 JOE BECOMES MR. FIXIT

Carpooling with Engineers

When I was working at the Lisle Plant, I was in a car pool with two other engineers. We always talked about fixing things in our new homes. It was almost like a contest to see who fixed the most difficult problem. So whenever something broke in my house, I saw it as a challenge to see if I could find and fix the problem as cheaply as possible. In most cases I was able to make simple repairs for very little money. Here are some cases in point.

Joe the Repairman

One day at work I got a call from MaryAnne that the washing machine was leaking water on the basement floor and she wanted to buy a new one. I told her to let me look at it before we bought a new one. When I got home from work, she told me Sears had a brand new washing machine waiting for us at the store. I said again let me look at it. So after dinner I went down to the basement to check it out. I saw that it was leaking so I laid it on its front so I could look at the bottom of the machine and see if I could see where the leak was coming from. I saw water on a small piece of rubber which was part of a pump. I told MaryAnne I was going to the Sears parts store to see if they had the rubber thing. When I got to the store, they did indeed have the rubber thing and it only cost one dollar. So I got two. I replaced the rubber thing in about five minutes and the leak was fixed. All I needed to fix it was a screwdriver to remove and replace the screws holding the rubber thing. So I saved the cost of a new washer or a service call for the low cost of one dollar. A few years later, we had another leak and this time I had the other rubber thing on hand and I fixed it again.

Joe the MAYTAG Repairman

Another time the washer would not pump the water out of the tub. So MaryAnne wanted to replace the washer again. Again I told her to let me look at it and see what I could do. This time I was stumped. So I called the MAYTAG store and told the guy about my problem. He suggested that something might be blocking the drain hose. So I checked it and sure enough, there was a dryer sheet blocking the drain hose. I removed the dryer sheet and the problem was fixed. This fix didn't cost me any money at all.

Joe Repairs the Dryer

After I married Dawn, the dryer would not dry the clothes. So I checked and saw that the gas was not being ignited so the dryer was not getting hot. I went to the MAYTAG store and told the guy about my problem. He said that there were three relays that could cause the problem and each one was $15. He also said a service call was $100. So I bought the three relays and replaced all three of them myself and I fixed the problem for $45 instead of calling a serviceman out to replace one bad relay at a cost of $100 (for the service call) + $15 (for the bad relay) or $115.

Joe Replaces the Ice Maker

A couple of years ago, the ice maker on our fridge went out. So I bought a new one and planned to replace it myself. When I got home, I was unable to remove the electrical wires from the old ice maker.

Dawn suggested that I see if there was a YouTube video on how to replace our icemaker. I checked and sure enough, there was a video available and we watched it as it showed the trick to removing the wires from the old ice maker. Then I replaced it with no more problems and it has been working great ever since. Thanks YouTube and Dawn.

Joe Tells Michael How to Fix the Heat/Air Problem

On one occasion when we were living in our second house, I was on a road trip and called home to let them know I made it to my destination. They told me that the house was cold and they couldn't make the heat turn on. I had replaced the thermostat with a new set-back thermostat so that it could turn the heat down during the day while we were at work and the kids were in school. I determined that the new thermostat must have died. So I told the family to put Michael on the phone. I told Michael that he was going to fix the problem by replacing the new thermostat with the original one. I told him to get a screwdriver and follow my instructions. I told him to turn off the power and move the five wires from the defective thermostat to the old thermostat. I told him to move them one by one instead of taking all of them off and trying to put all five back on right again. He did just as I told him and his older siblings were amazed when he fixed the problem by doing what I said. Michael saved the day and he was only in grammar school at this time. When I got home, I returned the defective thermostat for a good one and installed the new one and we had no more problems with it.

Joe Does a Brake Job

One Saturday while still living in my first house I decided to get a brake job on my car. A store about 20 miles or so from my house was having a sale on brake jobs. So I got up early so I could be there when they opened to get my $40 brake job.

When the store opened I rushed in and told them what I wanted. They asked if I had an appointment. I told them that there was nothing in the newspaper ad about an appointment. They said if I left the car there all day that they might be able to get to it. But I couldn't do that because I needed my car to get home. So I left with no brake job.

On the way home I decided to buy the new brake shoes and do it myself. I knew my friend Ron Zarn could help me and I knew he did his own brake jobs. When I got home, I called Ron and he said he had to finish doing some things and then he would come over.

I went to the garage and decided to wait for Ron. While waiting, I thought to myself that I would get my jack out of the trunk and jack up my car so it is already up when he gets here. So I did.

While I was waiting, I got another idea. I said I knew I could take the tire off by removing the lug nuts. Then he could get right to the brakes on one side of the car. So I took off the lug nuts and the tire.

Then I sat down to wait for Ron. As I was looking at the brakes, I thought that surely I can remove the old brakes. I just had to loosen a couple of springs and the brakes would come right off. I thought anyone can do that and so that's what I did.

Ron still didn't show up. So I thought that I got the old brakes off without much trouble, certainly I could put the new ones back on in their place and replace the springs. So I did.

Guess what. I just replaced the brakes on one side of my car. So I put the tire back on and lowered the jack. Then I thought if I could do one side, why not the other. So I did it.

When Ron showed up, I told him what I did. He was surprised. While he was there, he offered to adjust the emergency brake for me and the job was done. It was not even noon yet and the job was done. I think we celebrated with some lunch.

The key to doing this job was I believed that I could do each little component part of the job. Then in doing all the little jobs correctly, I completed the big job. Remember that if you think you can do something, you can do it and if you think you can't do something, then you can't do it because you don't try.

Joe the Plumber

One day I got a call from MaryAnne and she said our hot water heater was leaking water all over the floor. So I went home and low and behold, my hot water heater was leaking water all over the floor. So I knew the thing to do was turn off the water to the hot water heater to stop the leaking. Then I could go out and buy a new hot water heater with the same size and pipe arrangement and replace the old one with the new one.

But first I had to turn the water off. The builder had conveniently located a shut off valve in the pipe bringing the water to top of the hot water heater. All I had to do was turn the valve until the leaking stopped. So I tried turning it with my hand but I couldn't budge it.

No problem says I. I have a nice big wrench that can turn anything. So I cleverly fit my wrench around the valve and pulled on the wrench. SNAAAAP! I just snapped the shutoff valve right off its stem. Now what am I going to do.

"No problem" I said to myself. The shutoff for the whole house is right next to the hot water heater. All I have to do is turn the shutoff valve and shutoff the water for the whole house until I can replace the hot water heater.

So I reached down and tried to turn the valve. It wouldn't budge. "No problem" said I as I reached for my trusty wrench that just broke the first valve. So I put my wrench on the valve and turned it. SNAAAAP! I just snapped the whole house shutoff valve right off its stem. Now what am I going to do?

Fortunately, there is a shutoff valve outside the house in the parkway. So I came to my senses and called the city water dept. and asked them to turn off the water to my house from the outside. So they dug a hole down to the valve and shutoff the water to the house. Now we have no running water and only one flush left for each toilet. However, the lack of water pressure did slow down the leak in the hot water heater.

So I went to the plumbing store and bought a new whole house water shutoff valve. The one in my house was soldered into the supply line and could not be easily removed. So I got my first brilliant idea of the day. I looked at the new shutoff valve and realized that I could take it apart and remove the guts of the valve which I did. Then I did the same with the broken valve. Then I replaced the guts of the original valve with the guts of the new valve and now I could turn the water on and off for the entire house without using the outside valve.

So I called the water company and they turned my water back on for the house. Before calling them I turned the new valve to the off position and that's when I realized that I had been turning all the previous valves in the wrong direction. They were already open and I was attempting to open them further with the help of my trusty wrench. Dumb. Dumb. Dumb.

Next I went to the store and purchased a new hot water heater and replaced the old one with the new one. I attached the water pipes and the gas line and then turned on the water to the house. Thank God it didn't leak. So I could leave the water to the house on and we now had hot and cold running water (after the heater warmed up) and toilets we could flush. And it was only midnight when I got to bed that night or was it morning. I can't remember if I ever did replace that valve on the new hot water heater. I think I finally did get around to it one day.

Did I happen to mention that I am not much of a plumber, just in case the reader didn't figure that out yet?

Joe the Plumber Strikes Again

On another occasion, I came home from work to find that the main toilet in the house was plugged up and wouldn't flush properly. Fixing plugged toilets is just the kind of job I like to do right before dinner.

So I got out my trusty toilet router and attempted to unblock the toilet. Needless to say that didn't work. I tried the mighty plunger with similar results. No what do I do? Calling a plumber was totally out of the question. So I decided to remove the toilet and take it out to the yard where I could see the bottom of the toilet. So I removed the toilet tank. Then I removed the bolts holding the toilet to the floor. Lastly, I carried the toilet out to the yard where I could hit it with the garden hose. After all that, a bar of soap comes sliding out of the toilet. About that time my son Michael comes out to the yard and sees the bar of soap and exclaims "Dad. You found my boat!" Needless to say, Michael and I had a little talk about his playing Navy in the toilet. However, after only a couple of hours and lots of work, I saved the cost of a plumber coming to our house.

CHAPTER 12 GOODBYE MARYANNE, HELLO DAWN

MaryAnne Brozovich 1946 - 1988

On September 9, 1988, I got up early and went to work out at my executive fitness class at Illinois Benedictine College. When I arrived home after my work out, I noticed that Amy and Michael had already gone to school. They must have gotten a ride from one of the neighbors. I went to our bedroom to shower and I noticed MaryAnne was blue and unresponsive in our bed. Since 9-1-1 was not invented yet, I got a phone book and called for an ambulance. I am sure it took me several minutes to find the right number to call. I even called at least one wrong number before getting through to the fire department. They arrived fairly quickly and determined that MaryAnne had died that morning. Someone asked if I wanted to see a priest and I said yes. He arrived very quickly. By then the older kids were up and still at home. I was asked what to do with MaryAnne's body. I believe the priest recommended an undertaker and I called him. In a little while, the undertaker came and took MaryAnne's body to the funeral home. The older kids and I went out to the patio and talked to the priest while the undertaker removed the body. The priest was quite comforting and everyone was pretty calm. Apparently, MaryAnne had suffered a fatal heart attack.

Later, I called off of work and went to the funeral home to make the arrangements for MaryAnne. I had to pick out the casket, contribute her information for the newspaper notice, purchase some flowers and select the music for her funeral mass. Then I called everyone I could think of and told them what happened. I spoke to the folks at St. Joan of Arc and they told me I should probably come and get the Amy and Michael. Amy was 11 and Michael was 7 at this time. That afternoon Joanne picked them up and told them what happened and everything would be okay.

Neighbors brought us food and came over to share some stories about their good times with MaryAnne. It was a very sad time for all of us. A few days later, we had a funeral mass for MaryAnne at St. Joan of Arc Church. I think there were about 30 cars in her funeral procession. Many of our friends, relatives, and work colleagues attended. She was laid to rest at a small cemetery in Naperville.

One of the people who attended the funeral service was my brother's sister-in-law, Bonnie. She and I had gone to the same high school but never met until after my brother started dating her sister. Ironically, a few months later, my kids and I attended Bonnie's funeral.

Life after MaryAnne

By now I got a new assignment at AT&T. I was teaching computer programming and computer networking for AT&T at the Hickory Ridge Conference Center in Lisle. I was very sad at this time. I would go to lunch and after getting my food, I would sit at a corner table by myself facing the corner walls in the dining room. I really didn't want to talk to anybody then.

Life went on as usual at home. Fortunately, my daughter Joanne was 21 and the twins were 20 and they were all going to college. However, they were able to help me keep an eye on Amy and Michael after MaryAnne's death.

My job required me to do some traveling but I tried to keep my travel to a minimum at this time in my life. My older kids did a great job of helping me care for Amy and Michael. We got them to school on time every day and we all chipped in to help them with their homework when they needed help. My daughter Joyce kind of took Amy under her wing and took Amy with her when she went places. I often took Michael to the park so he could run around and burn off some of his unlimited supply of energy.

My friend Tom Melton was a big consolation to me during this time. One time after MaryAnne died,

I went fishing with him at his place in Wisconsin. While fishing we talked a lot about MaryAnne and what I should do next. He was a great listener.

Joe and the Single Professionals

One Sunday in the spring of 1989, I went to St. Joan of Arc Church with my kids. At some point, the priest mentioned that there would be a meeting for people going through grief. It was for people who lost a loved one or people who were going through a divorce. So I went. While there I met a woman who told me about an organization for college-educated men and women looking for partners called Single Professionals. So I went to a few meetings and got to know some of the people there.

The first meeting I attended was at a lady's house where we prepared a bunch of invitations to be sent to all the members. Another time, I went to Four Lakes Pub for a breakfast meeting. There I met women who were teachers, accountants, and other college-degreed positions. I met a lady there and we ended up going to an outing in Wisconsin where we did some tubing and canoeing on a small river. It was fun for me and gave me something to do instead of just sitting at home and watching my kids.

The next event I attended was a big meeting in a Holiday Inn to hear a speaker talk about meeting people. She gave a nice talk and then invited all of us to introduce ourselves to members of the opposite sex. I saw a nice looking young lady and introduced myself and started talking to her. She told me her name was Dawn. We finished our conversation and then I said "Good bye" and went home. Until we finally said good bye, I never realized that women were lining up to meet me and guys were lining up to meet her. So I met even more women that night. On the way home it suddenly occurred to me that I never even got Dawn's phone number or any other contact information. I knew I liked her but asking for her phone number never occurred to me.

A week or so later, the Single Professionals sponsored a dance for members at a local hotel. I went to the dance hoping to find Dawn. I met a lot of women that night and danced with many of them. Dawn said hi to me but she spent most of the night dancing with some guy on the other side of the dance floor. So I just danced with the women who were on my side of the dance floor.

When they announced the last dance for the evening, Dawn and I were on the same side of the dance floor and Dawn's mom suggested that we dance the last dance together. We both agreed and enjoyed our first dance together. When the dance ended, we exchanged business cards and wrote our home numbers on them for each other. Then I asked her if she wanted to go to a nearby Denny's for some coffee and/or dessert. She accepted and we had a great time talking and learning more about each other. She told me that she was a tax accountant for Allstate Insurance Company and lived in Arlington Heights. I told her I was an engineer for AT&T and lived in Woodridge. I also told her that I couldn't figure out how I got the prettiest girl at the dance to leave with me.

After that night, I called Dawn often. Then we had several dates for dinner, movies, plays and other fun things. I felt like I was a teenager in high school again. Dawn was 15 years younger than me but it didn't bother her and it sure didn't bother me. I would usually see Dawn for dinner on Friday nights. A flower shop in our area sold single roses for one dollar each on Friday nights. So I would always buy Dawn one single rose when I went to see her on Friday nights. She would put them in a vase and one rose would generally last almost a whole week before I replaced it with another one dollar rose. She loved them and she didn't even mind when I told her how inexpensive they were.

On New Year's Eve in 1989, I took Dawn to Jerry Sharko's restaurant in Lombard for dinner. It was a very nice place and we enjoyed a wonderful meal plus a couple of glasses of wine. After eating I started a sentence with "Someday we ought to get married…" Dawn interrupted me and said "Are you asking?" I thought and thought before I answered. I really didn't plan to propose that night but what was I going to do? So about one second later I said "Yup. I'm asking." She said "I accept." Since I wasn't planning on proposing I didn't have a ring or anything to give her. However, she didn't seem to mind. We went ring shopping a few weeks later and I got Dawn an engagement ring and a wedding ring and she got me a wedding ring.

When we came home from dinner, we told the kids about our plan to be married. We agreed that the following June would be a good time. The kids seemed less than thrilled with the idea. I guess they weren't ready for Dawn to replace their mom. However, MaryAnne had died about a year and four months prior to our engagement and we had dated exclusively for about seven months before our engagement. So we were okay with it and we figured that they would adjust since Dawn was a wonderful person and loved kids. Eventually, the kids did come to love Dawn, but things were a little rough in the beginning.

Wedding Day Arrives

We set our wedding date on June 9, 1990 at St. Joan of Arc Church in Lisle, Illinois. All my kids were in the wedding party and Dawn's sister, Alexandria, was her maid of honor. It was a beautiful sunny day in Lisle that day. I think the service began around 11:00 a.m. We had a small wedding with about 40 people. My lifelong friend Joe Hrstich was my best man. Dawn's cousins from Indiana were there as well as her father from Arkansas and her mom from Missouri. The ceremony was short and sweet and we got lots of pictures to commemorate the event. We went to the Lisle Hilton for lunch and cocktails. We liked it so much we spent the night there. Everyone else got to go home while it was still light outside.

Honeymoon in Hawaii

We got married in June but that was a busy time for Dawn at work so we postponed our honeymoon until September. When September came we flew first class to Hawaii thanks to all the United flying miles I accumulated with my AT&T business trips. Flying first class is great, especially when you are flying for 9 hours. The seats are like recliners and there are only two seats side by side instead of three like there is in coach. The food and wine were fabulous.

When we landed in Honolulu, it was around 5:00 p.m. in Hawaii but our bodies told us it was 10:00 p.m. in Chicago. So instead of going to bed at 5:00 in the afternoon, we forced ourselves to stay up until around 11:00 p.m. Hawaii time which was 5:00 a.m. on our body clocks. The next morning our bodies were adjusted to Hawaii time and we could function normally again.

We spent the first three days of our honeymoon in Honolulu. While we were there, we went sightseeing on the island of Oahu. We saw the Arizona memorial and the USS Bowfin Museum and Park at Pearl Harbor, the Polynesian Cultural Center, a pineapple plantation, and lots of other neat stuff.

On the third day, we boarded our ship for a cruise around the islands. When we arrived at each port we would have breakfast on the ship and then we called the rental car company and they picked us up from the boat dock and took us to the rental car place at the airport. There we rented a car for the day and went sightseeing on each island. At the end of the day, we returned the car at the airport and the rental car folks gave us a ride back to the dock. We had dinner on the ship and went to bed. While we were sleeping, the ship sailed to the next island. The next morning we woke up and did the same thing at the next island. We did this every day except for the first day when we stayed at sea all day.

When we were on the islands we noticed a place called Hilo Hatti's. Every island had at least one. We went there to buy clothes, souvenirs, jewelry, etc. The unique thing about the place was the fact that they had a place for the spouses of shoppers to rest while their partners shopped. In a little resting room, they had a TV and VCR with lots of video tapes of Hawaii plus cool drinks for those of us who were tired of shopping. I loved that place. Dawn could shop all day and I didn't mind. I was happy watching video tapes about Hawaii. I never understood why other stores didn't do this.

When we were taking in the sights on one island, we noticed that we were practically the only ones at this tourist location. I thought that was odd. Then the bus from the ship arrived with a crowd of tourists from the ship as we were leaving. We realized that these shore excursions from the ship brought a crowd with them everywhere they went. When we mentioned our experience to the people we had dinner with on the ship, they asked if they could come with us in the rental car. We said okay and the four of us went sightseeing together for the next couple of days. We split the cost of the car 50-50 so our $30/day rental car only cost us $15 per couple. The shore excursions were much more expensive but they did include meals.

While on the ship, I noticed lots of people celebrating their 25th and 50th wedding anniversaries. Some were in really bad shape physically. Some had oxygen tanks and many were in wheelchairs. We were glad we decided to go to Hawaii while were still young and able to enjoy our vacation.

On one occasion, the captain of the ship invited all the newlyweds to a private party. We had a great time and even got to talk to the captain. It was like we were living an episode of the "Love Boat".

On the last day we returned to Honolulu and caught our plane home. Again we flew first class. I mentioned to the airport personnel that on the way there, we sat in the back of the first class section and they were often out of the meal types that we would have preferred. So he gave us bulk head seats in first class. Have you ever sat in Row 1? It was really nice.

We had a great trip home but when we got to Chicago, they couldn't find our luggage. So we went home without it. A few days later they brought our bags to our house. Apparently, our luggage got shipped to Japan. However, we did finally get it and nothing was missing. It was a good thing that they lost it on the way back rather than on the way there. In spite of losing our luggage, we still had a wonderful time on our Hawaiian Honeymoon.

Living in Our New Home on Greene Road

After we got married, we decided to move to a bigger and different home to make a fresh start. We found a builder that was building homes in a new sub-division called "Seven Bridges", named after the seven bridges over the nearby DuPage River. We found a model that we liked and could afford and had the builder make it for us. We also found a nice lot to put it on. While we were still deciding which lot we wanted, there was a big storm and some of the lots close to the DuPage River had lakes in what would be their back yards. So when we picked our lot, we got one far from the river. I found out later that it was one of the highest lots in the subdivision. This turned out to be a great idea when we got 17 inches of rain in one night. The people near the river got water in their basements and had to throw out their carpeting, wallboard, furniture, appliances, and everything else that got soaked by the flood waters. We could see huge dumpsters filled with this stuff as we rode through our neighborhood after the storm. We didn't get a drop of water in our basement. We had a sump pump but it never ran during this deluge or any other time as far as I know.

Note to self: Always build or buy your home on the highest lot in the immediate area.

One of my co-workers who lived in the area just bought a brand new Cadillac. On the day after the big storm, he decided to drive through what he thought was a puddle of water on the road. Well the puddle was in a low spot in the road and when he tried to drive through it, his car stalled. I suspect water got into his engine. He got out of his car to walk home and get his second car to pull or push his Cadillac out of the "puddle". When he got out of the car, the water was up to the bottom of the door. When he got back the water was up to his seat and his new Cadillac was half full of water. He called his insurance man and his insurance company declared the car a total loss.

Note to self: Don't try to drive through big "puddles" after a huge rain storm.

Dawn's sister lived in a nearby subdivision which had a lake located in the center. As the rain fell, the lake grew and grew. By the time the rain stopped, the lake had made it to their garage and if it had risen another couple of inches, it would have flooded their entire basement which was below the level of the garage floor. Fortunately, the rain stopped before they took on any more water.

Dawn and I had only been married about six months when we moved into our new home on Greene

Road in November of 1990. Our new home had five bedrooms and three bathrooms. So each kid had his or her own bedroom (Joanne, Joyce, Mike and Amy). See picture below. I invited my son Joe to use the den as the sixth bedroom. He declined and moved out to find himself an apartment which he was able to do. He was the first bird to leave the nest but certainly not the last.

Trick on Dawn Backfires

One day after we moved into our new home, one of my darling children, namely Joanne, decided to play a trick on Dawn. She put a rubber band around the sprayer in the sink so that Dawn would get soaked when she turned the water on. Unfortunately for Joanne, she was the first one to turn on the water and she got soaked. We all had a good laugh about that and no one tried to play that trick again.

Michael is Diagnosed with A.D.D.

Michael went to St. Joan of Arc Catholic School through fifth grade. He had difficulty staying on task and getting his work done. He hated reading, writing, and most other school subjects. He also hated sitting in one place for hours on end. So I took him to a pediatric neurologist and had him tested. They told me he had A.D.D. (Attention Deficit Disorder) which caused his problems in school. I asked the doctor what kind of work he could do when he got older. The doctor said he would make a good salesman and he could probably do any job where he could be on his feet moving around. The counselor at St. Joan suggested that we move him to a public school that had more resources to help him. So we put him in John F. Kennedy Junior High for his 6th, 7th and 8th grades. Michael seemed to do okay at Kennedy. The counselors were very nice to him and spent some time with him trying to help him with his issues.

Knowing he would probably not go on to college, I tried to get him into courses that could lead to a career. One of the classes he took at Kennedy was a class where they built things and did simple home repairs. He and his partner built a wall with both inside and outside corners. Then they had to apply drywall to their wall. Then they put in a light switch and maybe an outlet. His wall looked pretty good by the time we saw it at an open house.

CHAPTER 13 LIFE IN THE 1990S

Michael Helps Dad Remodel the Basement

Since he showed an interest in building walls, I had a great idea. I got him to help me finish our basement. The main thing I wanted to do was to build a room that he could play in. So he helped me build the walls. Then we put in electrical outlets about every eight feet or so along the walls. Next we put in a wood floor. We got a 22 caliber nail gun to put the nails into our concrete floor below our wood floor. It looked like the handle of a hammer with a hole in the bottom to hold the nail/bullet. We would strike the top of the tube with a hammer to fire the nail/bullet into the concrete. He liked that a lot although his friends in school wouldn't believe that I would let him use it.

We put in a drop ceiling with florescent lights. We put insulation into walls that were adjacent to the outside walls of the basement. I used 5/8 inch wood paneling or what I called barn siding for the walls. I had fixed so many holes in the walls in my first house that I defied him to make a hole in this stuff. Then we got wall to wall carpeting for our room. I think I had that installed by professionals because I didn't have a way to stretch the carpet. We even made a closet with shelves where he could put his toys and games. Our room was complete. We had fun building it and Mike learned how to do all these things.

Michael Grows Up

When Michael went to High School, we signed him up for all the hands on courses we could find. One course had his class build a house from scratch with real home construction guys. Each day they would leave school for a couple of hours and go to the home site. They laid the foundation, built the walls, did the electrical work, plumbing, carpeting, roofing, and everything else that goes into a house from foundation to roof. He liked that course too.

He also took a course in woodworking and made some nice things using the equipment they had. Most important, he learned how to operate all those machines safely.

When Michael grew up and graduated from high school he did indeed become a good salesman. He worked for Lowe's, Firestone, an alarm company, a furniture store, and a few other places while he was trying to figure out what it was that he really wanted to do. Now he has a job where he works with his hands and repairs broken machinery. In his spare time, he has his own business installing flat screen TVs on walls, fireplaces, on their decks or patios, and anywhere else customers want them. He turned out to be a wonderful guy and a great husband and father to his three girls.

Michael wrote me the following letter for my 70th birthday. Here it is just the way he wrote it.

Michael's Letter to Dad

For my Dad

dad so many memories to remember.

All the things in life that I have from skills, to memories, working with others overcoming objections, and finding solutions. I attest a lot of what I have to you. Starting out at a very young age I understood how really important you were and still are to our family. As head of the household now I only can hope to be as good as a father to my kids as you were and still are to us. From teaching me how to change oil and tires on Stonewall to learning how to ride my bike (right into that bush at the end of the driveway) and how not to stop my bike by dragging my shoes and having to get replacements all the time. I remember you teaching me how to pull wire and wire in electrical outlets on Green Road house. I use the skills every day in my field career and business ownership. As an adult I never would have thought that what I was taught at such a young age would be such an instrumental part of my development and success as an adult. Learning how to frame walls how to do light electrical work and just grow as a person I never realized how important all of those things that you taught me. I go through my daily routine and up until recently I never realized how my daily routine wouldn't be if I didn't have you as my father. I remember I used to call you all the time at work (630.224.2364) and ask you questions how do I do this? How do I spell that? When you come home can you help me with this? I remember how you got the Microsoft bookshelf to help me with big projects at school like the family tree project (that you still have). I understand now as an adult how difficult I must have been as a son. Rebellions telling you that I know everything, very rude and unreasonable. I realize that I truly have grown because of your teachings and I see and hear stories every day about parents who are giving up on their kids and not having the advantages that I had. Being the youngest of 5 kids I realize just how hard you worked on me. you never gave up you always tried to find ways to help me whether it was spending more time with me by, going fishing, finding a doctor for me to talk to, becoming involved in my extracurricular activities like Boy Scouts, working side by side with me on school projects. I would always look forward to our fishing trips to Wisconsin. We always would try catch big northern pike but normally just fill the live well with perch and croppies. I realize now how wonderful and lucky I am to have a father that would do that when I hear so many stories of parents just walking away. I am 1 of 6 kids but I feel as if I was a spoiled single child. Thanks for all the great memories and I hope for more and more.

Happy Belated Birthday.

I started this email when you had mentioned the idea and finally finished it sorry I didn't have it for you on your birthday but I felt that something like this I really needed to take the time to remember everything.

Michael J Brozovich
Sr A/V Installer/Sales Rep
www.thetvpro.com

I wrote the following letter to Michael for his 35th birthday.

Joe's Letter to Son Michael

Happy Birthday Michael!!

Can you believe that you are 35 years old? Where did the time go?

Since you wrote a nice letter to me, I thought it might be appropriate for me to write one to you. I was worried about you when you were little and diagnosed with A.D.D. I wondered and worried about what would happen to you when you became an adult. I worried more when you didn't go to college. However, you showed me that I had nothing to worry about. You got some jobs and supported yourself very quickly after graduating from high school. Although the jobs did not last long, you always managed to get another one that was better than the last one. The current job seems to be the best of all the jobs you ever had and the folks there seem to like and trust you. I saw that when they paid your way to New York City to help the customer install your product.

I can also see that The TV Pro is also quite successful. I am sure that is because you know what you are doing and work very hard at it and your customers see and appreciate your efforts.

I also see one other very important thing about you. You help everybody that needs your help. Whenever your brother or sisters need help with some project, they call you and you respond. You have helped every single one of them in more ways than I can count. You also helped me with my stuff. FYI: This is what Jesus did when he was here. He fed the hungry, cured the blind and lame; raised Lazarus from the dead and much more.

I can also see that you are much loved by your wife and daughters and even your animals. I call that success any way you measure it.

Today on your 35th birthday and every day I want you to know how very proud I am to be your dad. Success is measured in many different ways. I thought I would just share my favorite poem with you.

"What is success?

To laugh often and much;
To win the respect of intelligent people and the affection of children;
To earn the appreciation of honest critics and endure the betrayal of false friends;
To appreciate beauty, to find the best in others;
To leave the world a bit better, whether by a healthy child, a garden patch or a redeemed social condition;
To know even one life has breathed easier because you have lived.
This is to have succeeded.

--- Inaccurately attributed to Ralph Waldo Emerson

Love you,

Dad

Amy's Letter to Dad for his 72nd Birthday

Hi Dad,

Since you recently shared my birthday story with me, I thought it would be fun to share 72 memories with you! So here goes:

1. Fishing at 55th Street Park
2. Dairy Queen desserts for crossing the monkey bars
3. Sharing weekends at the "Party Park"
4. Learning to ride my bike with your help
5. Watching Saturday morning cartoons on the couch together
6. Eating your famous butter and jelly breakfast sandwiches
7. Traveling to WI for week long fishing trips
8. Chasing Frogs at Franks on Lake Chetak
9. Fishing from the boat with Pudgy scaring all the fish
10. You announcing, "Everyone duck, Michael is going to cast"

11. *The boat reaching "Ramming Speed" as we searched for the hole in the lake*

12. *You joining me for curriculum night at SJA in my first grade class*

13. *You being a guest speaker for "When I grow up day"*

14. *You reminding me that I can do whatever I want, if I work hard.*

15. *You telling us we can have as many dogs as we want when we move out!*

16. *You leading the pack that filled up the pew at church*

17. *You driving the wagon from IN when visiting Uncle Mike or Grandma B*

18. *You and I on the ride to Appleton to see Uncle John before he moved out*

19. *You sharing different ideas about Jesus and our faith*

20. *Pizza, pizza night from Little Caesars - when two pizzas came side by side*

21. *You repairing holes in the walls at our Stonewall house*

22. *Our vacation to Florida with Mike and Joyce in 1988*

23. *Catching every show the magic kingdom had to offer*

24. *"Traveling" through the different countries at Epcot Center*

25. *Introducing us to a garbage disposal at the hotel*

26. *You helping us through mom's death*

27. *Your famous spaghetti dinner nights*

28. *Spending weekends in the pool on Stonewall while you cut the grass*

29. *You taking and picking me up from Ms. Dotti's Dance studio*

30. *You operating giant VHS camcorders at my communion and dance shows*

31. *You and I sharing quiet rides to North early in the morning*

32. *You helping me with countless math problems*

33. *Your surprising us with a baby sister*

34. *You and I attending multiple parent teacher conferences*

35. *You teaching me to drive*

36. *High School Chorus Concerts with you in the audience*

37. *You cheering me on with the family when I graduated high school*

38. *You encouraging me through college courses*

39. *Countless conversations about what I should be when I grow up*

40. *Your encouragement when I decided to teach*

41. *Your pride shining through when I graduated with honors from COD*

42. *You taking me on college tours*

43. *Your dropping me off at Western University*

44. *Your trusting me with a car when I needed to escape from Western*

45. *Your support through the transfer to North Central College*

46. *Your enthusiasm at my college graduation*

47. Your helping me through financial decisions

48. Your becoming a proud grandpa, and holding JD at Olive Garden

49. You sharing your home with my family while visiting MO

50. JD first crawling, chasing your feet at the Nixa house

51. Chatting over a bowl of morning Cheerios with banana

52. Driving me in the caddie, as the bride-to-be, to St Margaret Mary

53. You walking me down the aisle - I'm the only girl you could do that for, so far!!

54. Adding ceiling fans and closets to our Hilton Head house

55. Building shelves and storage units for all our "stuff"

56. Helping us through Uncle Mike's departure from this world

57. Celebrating each of your subsequent grand children

58. Participating in their baptisms, communions, and sporting events

59. Playing in the Branson pools

60. Cakes and Crème treats while in Branson

61. Standing by grandma on her hardest of days

62. Sharing crepes in Colorado

63. Eating some great barbeque dinners

64. Sharing many German chocolate birthday cakes

65. Christmas masses and dinners with extended family

66. Leading the family in prayer

67. Working through new positions and challenges at work

68. Talking about "A-holes" at work and figuring out who they are and how to avoid them.

69. Offering encouragement and suggestions during unemployment

70. Supporting me in various diet initiatives – sometimes walking that road together

71. Guiding me to be a mother, daughter, and child of Christ

72. Loving me unconditionally every day!

Love you and looking forward to So Many More great memories :)

Love Amy Boz!

The Roll of Alcohol in My Life

When I was growing up, alcohol was rampant everywhere I went. My dad liked to drink beer and drank his share but I never saw him drunk. My mom really didn't drink much, if at all. When I went to Purdue in West Lafayette, Indiana, my friends and I would go to a bar/pizza place every Friday night and enjoy a pizza with pitchers of Carlings Black Label beer that only cost $1.00 per pitcher. Being the high rollers that we were, we took turns buying pitchers for everyone.

While working at the Western Electric Hawthorne Works, we would often have mixed drinks at lunch. That generally occurred when someone else was buying like a salesman trying to sell us something. On one occasion my colleagues and I thought we would go to the infamous Radar Lounge which was right across Cicero Avenue from the Hawthorne Works. We heard their sandwiches were really good so we thought we would try them. Since Hawthorne was a factory, hourly workers had to punch out for lunch so they couldn't leave until lunchtime officially started at 11:30 a.m. So we left a few minutes before that to avoid the rush and walked across the street around 11:25 a.m. When we walked in the door, we were the only ones there. However, the bar was setup with mixed drinks from end to end. We sat at a table and ordered our lunches. When the hourly workers came in, they all went to their pre-assigned seats at the bar and started enjoying their drinks. I recall a few of them had more than one drink. Having the drinks waiting for them allowed them to get loaded within the 30 minute lunch period. I wondered if their supervisors knew what was going on or if they went with them to the bar.

In the 1970s when I was working at the Western Electric Lisle plant, I probably drank more than I ever did in my life. It seemed like there was always something to celebrate and when we celebrated, we drank. On one of those occasions, we went to lunch at a bar that sold two drinks for the price of one. I think it may have been Christmas so we were not expected to return to work after lunch. So we just ate our lunches and had a couple of extra drinks. Then a waitress asked if we wanted to order more drinks before the two for one deal expired. I said "When does it end?" She said 8:00 p.m. I looked at my watch and it was almost 8:00 p.m. I had been drinking all afternoon and now I had to drive home because my car was there. How stupid was that? So I got in my car, pulled into the right lane and drove 30 mph all the way home. I shudder to think about what my blood alcohol level was while I was driving home that night. That was probably one of the stupidest things I ever did in my life.

Fortunately, over the course of my 33 year career, drinking alcohol slowly went away. I remember going out for lunch in my last year at work and all we ordered was pitchers of diet soda. Not one person even ordered a beer much less a mixed drink. And that happened whenever we went out for lunch. I don't know why it happened, but drinking alcohol at lunch just wasn't done any more.

One of my colleagues from work retired before me and continued to smoke and drink after his retirement. A few years ago he was diagnosed with cancer of the lungs. He went through chemotherapy and was declared cancer free. However, a few months later, the cancer came back. The doctor told him he had less than a week to live. His lungs were full of cancer and his kidneys and liver were destroyed by drinking. He died in a couple of days. Ironically, my friend was a big fan of John Wayne. When I read John Wayne's biography, I discovered that he died the same way as my friend.

Since I retired, I hardly ever drink any more except for maybe a glass of wine or beer when we go out to dinner. On rare occasions when we might buy a six pack of beer or a bottle of wine, we have it in our fridge for months before we finally finish it. I don't miss it a bit. I only wish I had stopped drinking sooner. I feel bad about setting a lousy example for my kids.

Amy Learns to Drive

In the early 1990s, Amy turned 15 and like all other kids, wanted to learn how to drive. So she got her permit and I was elected to be her instructor. So one morning, we got up early and I drove our 1990 Toyota Corolla around our neighborhood and showed her how easy it was to drive. The car was relatively small and easy to steer. So I finally stopped and let Amy take a turn at the wheel. Now I never expected that I had to tell her how to steer a car but I was wrong. She did know how to ride a bike, after all.

Amy got in the car, buckled her seat belt, turned it on and started driving. When we got to an intersection she decided to take a shortcut by driving over the curb and across the corner of a neighbor's lawn. At least one of the hub caps went flying off when she hit the curb. I told her to STOP and I retrieved the lost hubcap. Fortunately, the lawn was not damaged and Amy and I had a little talk wherein

I emphasized how important it was to keep the car on the road and not on our neighbors' lawns. She eventually figured that out and became a very good driver or, at least I didn't get any more bad reports about her driving.

Danielle Joins the Family

When Dawn and I got married, we were not planning on having any more children. I already had five and thought that was enough for anybody. However, God had other plans and Dawn and I got pregnant in 1992. On November 10th I took Dawn to Hinsdale Hospital and she gave birth to Danielle Marie at about 5:00 p.m. the following day. Both mother and baby were fine. We figured out that Danielle's birthday was exactly 271 days after Valentine's Day.

Danielle was seven pounds 13 ounces and 20 inches long. She was healthy and beautiful. The kids came to see their new sister the next day and everyone fell in love with Danielle when they saw her.

As Danielle grew older, we were afraid she was never going to learn how to walk. There was nothing physically wrong with her. It's just that her feet never hit the floor. Everyone wanted to hold her, feed her, change her and play with her.

Before Danielle was born the kids were not too crazy about Dawn. However, once Dani came along, they had to agree that maybe Dawn wasn't so bad after all.

Diversity Training for Joe

As I neared the end of my engineering career, I was asked to attend a lot diversity training sessions. That's where all Caucasian people are to assume blame for the plight of the African Americans in the U.S. I often wanted to say something in my own defense but never did. If I did, here is what I wanted to say. Just for the record let me share what I know about my family history. Both my parents grew up in poor families. My mother's parents owned a farm in Croatia and never had any slaves to my knowledge or any power over them or even any opportunity to discriminate against them. In fact, I doubt that my mother even saw an African American until she got to this country at the age of 21.

To my knowledge, my father's parents never owned a home or any slaves. They never had any power to discriminate against any African Americans or mistreat them. My parents never owned or mistreated any African Americans or anyone else for that matter. Like many other people in my era, my family was poor, hard-working, and earned whatever they managed to accumulate. They never took anything from anybody or mistreated anyone or discriminated against anyone that I ever saw or heard of. So when some people tend to blame all white people for the plight of some minorities, may I respectfully exempt myself and my family that notion?

Furthermore, there were no rich plantation owners living on the East Side of Chicago when I was there. All the fathers of guys I knew worked in the steel mills, the General Mills plant, the Ford Motor Company plant, or loading and unloading ships. Everybody I knew was blue collar except for my doctor, dentist, and lawyer. None of these people were in a position to discriminate against anyone even if they wanted to. My generation and I fall in the same boat. There were no minorities in my grammar school or my high school when I went there except for one Hispanic boy. I never saw anyone do anything unkind to him or hurt him. I knew of no minorities living on the East Side of Chicago while I was growing up there. So place the blame where it is due and please leave the rest of us alone. Amen.

Just so you don't think I am some crazy racist, let me share some personal things with the readers. I had the good fortune to work with and associate with many minority friends and colleagues. My daughter married a Mexican man. My son married a Philippine woman. My brother married an African American woman. Four of my seven grandchildren have one minority parent. So discrimination is not now, nor has it ever been, a problem in my family.

Joe and his Team Earn a U.S. Patent

In the early 1990s I was working at the Hickory Ridge Training Center teaching courses on AT&T products. About that time, we got word that the training center wasn't making enough money and therefore it was being closed ASAP. We were all encouraged to find other jobs within AT&T. I saw that an old friend of mine named Paul Simek who was looking for people to work on the 9-1-1 project. I asked him what he wanted me to do for him and he said make an ISDN PSAP or Integrated Services Digital Network Public Safety Answering Point.

I asked "What is that?"

He said "I don't know, but you are going to tell me what it is after you invent it."

I need to say a little bit about the existing PSAPs (that's where 9-1-1 calls are answered) before talking about our invention.

The problem with 9-1-1 at that time was it took too long to complete a 9-1-1 call. 9-1-1 callers were getting frustrated and hanging up and calling back repeatedly. In the meantime, someone may be dying right in front of them.

The reason the calls took so long was that the phone system had to figure out where to send the 9-1-1 call and then send it there. For instance, if someone dials a 9-1-1 in Chicago, the call has to go to the Chicago PSAP. If another person dials the same three digits, 9-1-1, in Orlando, Florida, the call needs to go to the Orlando PSAP. If someone dials 9-1-1 from a rural county in Missouri, the call will probably be sent to the local sheriff's office.

So the phone system has to figure out where the call is coming from so it knows to send the call to the PSAP nearest to the caller. Then when it knows where to send it, it has to send the call to the phone system at the PSAP which in turn, rings the phone on the call taker's desk.

When the call taker answers the call, he sees the caller's location and the names and phone numbers of the three emergency service providers for the caller. The three services are Police, Fire and Emergency Medical Services. This information also must be sent to the PSAP.

The call takers generally answer 9-1-1 calls with the words "9-1-1, what is your emergency?" Then they will transfer the call to the emergency service provider. Since most calls are for the police, the 9-1-1 calls generally go to a police facility where they can dispatch officers to the location needing assistance.

So our patent was about saving time in the above scenario. Instead of sending the call to another phone system, like the one at the police station, we provided the ISDN PSAPs with phones directly off the telephone switch handling the call. Then that switch can ring the PSAP's phones directly (just like any other phone) without the extra step of signaling the local switch to have it ring the PSAP phone.

To make a long story short, phone companies tested our new PSAP concept and we did indeed save several precious seconds of time delivering the calls. This is a really big deal if someone is having a heart attack or a business is being robbed, for example. The sooner the service providers can get there, the higher likelihood that they can save the person or the business.

Our new PSAP not only delivered the call faster, it also delivered the names and phone numbers of all the caller's emergency services faster than the old system. There was a requirement that the display had to start displaying the location information and emergency service information within two seconds of the operator answering the 9-1-1 call. One of my jobs was to make that happen. Unbeknownst to me, when I finished writing the program to do that, my boss asked another member of our group to make sure my program met the 2 second requirement. His tests were designed to simulate a 48 position PSAP. He ran several tests and issued a report on his findings. My program exceeded the 2 second requirement in all test scenarios.

One unique feature of the ISDN PSAP was that the phone was totally controlled by a touch screen computer. The call taker had no access to the actual phone itself. Everything he or she needed to do could be done through this computer screen. The screen shot below shows what the 9-1-1 call taker sees when he or she answers your 9-1-1 call. This is taken from the patent. I suspect that this screen has changed considerably over the last 20+ years.

In 1999, the National Emergency Number Association (NENA) created and adopted a standard for ISDN PSAPs. You can read it at the URL below:

https://c.ymcdn.com/sites/www.nena.org/resource/collection/6EE32917-37BD-4FA0-838C-026931F702A6/NENA_04-003-v1_E9-1-1_ISDN_PSAP_Equipment_Utilizing_Basic_Rate_Interface.pdf

U.S. Patent   May 10. 1994   5,311,569

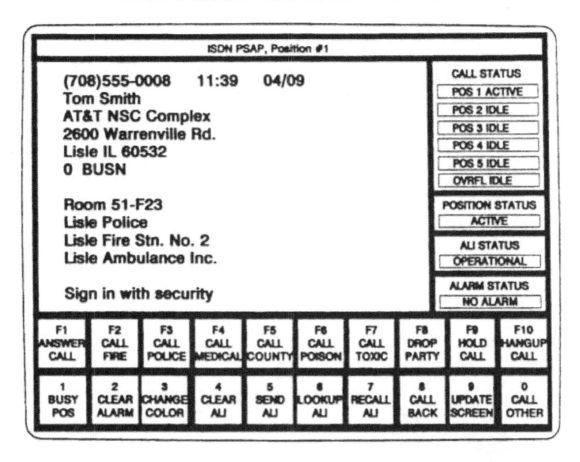

When I retired in 1998, ISDN PSAPs were deployed in Chicago and New York City as well as some smaller cities like Aurora, Illinois. All the people involved got credit for the patent. The patent was officially granted on May 10, 1994. The official name on our patent is "Line-Based Public Safety Answering Point 5,311,569". You can google that and read the patent for yourself. A Canadian Patent was also issued for our invention.

After we got our patents, I happen to get a chance to tour the Chicago 9-1-1 Center. I asked the tour guide if the system worked okay. He said that it worked great.

I was real glad to hear that. It is not often that some lowly engineers get a chance to do something that could potentially help hundreds or maybe thousands of other people. This was one such occasion. I am proud to say I was part of that project. It is just too bad this system was not available when MaryAnne died in 1988. Hopefully, others in similar situations will be rescued in time thanks to our invention. See patent information on the next page:

Line-Based Public Safety Answering Point

Joseph Michael Brozovich, et al

5,311,569
May 10, 1994

AT&T CORP.

The Commissioner of Patents and Trademarks

Has received an application for a patent for a new and useful invention. The title and description of the invention are enclosed. The requirements of law have been complied with, and it has been determined that a patent on the invention shall be granted under the law.

Therefore, this

United States Patent

Grants to the person or persons having title to this patent the right to exclude others from making, using or selling the invention throughout the United States of America for the term of seventeen years from the date of this patent, subject to the payment of maintenance fees as provided by law.

Harry F. Manbeck, Jr.

Commissioner of Patents and Trademarks

Melvina Gary
Attest

CHAPTER 14 JOE'S TEACHING CAREER

I always enjoyed getting in front of a group and teaching people useful things. I briefly considered getting my degree in education but I was told that engineers made a lot more money than teachers and didn't need to put up with unruly students in a classroom. So I majored in electrical engineering and did my teaching part time. Here's a brief summary of my teaching career.

College of DuPage

When I was eligible for a pension at AT&T, I thought about taking my pension and getting another full time job teaching. This was called double-dipping. So I applied at some local colleges including College of DuPage (COD). They offered me a part time job teaching electronics because their regular teacher was out on sick leave. I taught three different electronics classes in three consecutive school quarters. The hardest thing about this whole deal was that I had to prepare my lectures each time I taught a new course. This took a fair amount of time and I was still working full time at AT&T.

The classes I taught were both lab and lecture, so I had to grade the lab assignments, the homework and the tests. That was a lot of work for a part time job but it did give me a chance to pursue my teaching passion.

The best part about this job was that I was able to borrow electronics equipment from COD. On one occasion I borrowed an exhaust gas analyzer to adjust the carburetor on my car. The purpose of doing that was to get the best mixture of fuel and air for optimum performance and fuel efficiency. So while I was adjusting the mixture screws on the carburetor, the exhaust gas analyzer was reporting what was coming out of the tailpipe. If there was too much unburned fuel coming out, the air and gas mixture was too rich, so I needed to allow more air into the carburetor and vice versa. So I got my cars running well while I worked at COD and I enjoyed teaching there.

Illinois Benedictine College

In August of 1978 or 1979 my AT&T boss came up to me one morning and asked if I had my master's degree. I told him yes and he said Illinois Benedictine College (IBC) was looking for someone to teach a computer programming class starting in about a week. Apparently, the guy who was scheduled to teach it left just before the semester began. My boss said I needed to talk to the head of the Science Division who, at that time, was Dr. Rose Carney. I had a brief interview with her and she offered me the job. This was the start of my part-time teaching career which lasted about 30 years.

Shortly after I started, IBC decided to offer a Bachelor of Science Degree in Computer Science. Since several AT&T people were teaching there at the time, they invited us to help them write a grant to the National Science Foundation to purchase a computer system for the computer science program. We gladly obliged and a few months later, the grant was approved and IBC got their computer system.

I taught a number of different computer science classes for them and a few years later they awarded their first Bachelor of Science Degree in Computer Science to a very nice young lady who was in my very first class at IBC. I attended her graduation ceremony and her wedding.

One unexpected benefit of teaching there was my kids got 1/3 off their tuition while they attended there. So my daughter Joanne and my son Joe saved about $1000 per semester for each semester they were there. Joyce went to a junior college and later transferred to IBC to get her degree but I had left by then.

Teaching at IBC was a wonderful experience and it helped to prepare me to create and teach AT&T

classes at the Hickory Ridge Conference Center in Lisle. That experience also helped me launch my part-time math teaching career in Springfield, Missouri after I retired.

When Joanne was preparing to start her freshman year at IBC, we had to attend a parent orientation to IBC. So after working there several years, I went to the orientation at the gym. One set of parents got up and spoke about how great the school was and how the teachers really cared about the students. They said that one teacher in particular, spent a lot of time outside of the classroom to help their son pass the course he was struggling in. I recognized the name so I went to see the parents after their talk. I said "I think I may have had your son in one of my classes."

They said "What did you teach?"

I told them the class I taught and they said "You are the guy we were talking about." And thanked me profusely for all the help I gave their son.

I just got to school about an hour before my class started so I could see any students who needed my help. Their son came frequently and I helped him with his homework. I never dreamed it made such a big difference to him.

I never saw him again but I'm sure he became a success in life because he was a good kid and worked hard and was determined to get the correct answer.

Hickory Ridge Conference Center

Around 1985 I found that there was a job opening for an instructor at Hickory Ridge. I liked the idea of teaching there because it was very close to my house and it had a full fitness center with swimming pool for employees and guests. I interviewed for the job and got it. While I was there I taught computer programming classes and computer networking classes. AT&T taught these classes to educate their customers about their own products.

In addition to teaching classes, we, the instructors, also had to create the courses that we were going to teach. While I was developing new courses, desktop publishing became available on PCs and I jumped right on that. I liked working with computers and now I had a reason to have my own PC on my desk. So my group and I started creating our classes using PCs. I won an AT&T Technical Excellence Award for Outstanding Course Developer in 1989.

In addition to teaching and developing courses at Hickory Ridge, I was also required to take my classes to our customers and teach at their locations. This resulted in my taking a lot of trips to teach classes all over the country.'

Our group also got a request to work with the AT&T folks in North Carolina, to prepare and give a demonstration of our AT&T computer equipment to the U.S. Air Force personnel. They needed us to help AT&T land a big Air Force contract. That required me to travel to North Carolina for six straight weeks. I would come home on weekends, wash my clothes, and put them right back in my suitcase for the following week. MaryAnne stayed at home with the kids and held down the fort while I was gone. We did eventually win the Air Force contract so everyone was happy with our contribution to the overall success of that project.

I worked at Hickory Ridge from 1985 to 1991. So I was working there when MaryAnne died and when I met and married Dawn. I left Hickory Ridge in 1991 and joined the 9-1-1 group although I continued to work out at the Hickory Ridge fitness center until I retired and we moved to Missouri in 1999.

Springfield College and Robert Morris College

I lumped these two together because I taught the same course at both schools for one semester each. The course I taught was based on the MICROSOFT ACCESS® database. I taught it at Robert Morris College shortly before retiring and I taught it at Springfield College shortly after retiring. The only unique thing worth mentioning was that at Springfield College, the admin folks insisted that I keep impeccable attendance records. Apparently, some of the former students used school attendance as an alibi when they were accused of committing some crime. So teachers had to track the exact time they arrived to class and the exact time they left. I guess our attendance records were used in court cases prior to my teaching there.

If a student did not show up for class by the time class started, we were instructed to call him or her and find out their status. One time I called about a guy not showing up for class and his wife answered. I told her who I was and asked about him because he didn't show up for my class. Then she exploded and said "He told me he was going to class. When he gets home I am going to…" So I just said "Bye and have a nice day"

Ozarks Technical Community College

After retiring to Missouri in 1999, we joined a neighborhood Bible Study. At one of the meetings, a neighbor said she needed part time math instructors at a local community college known as Ozarks Technical Community College. I always loved math so I volunteered for the job. Later she officially interviewed me and I got the position. Another retired engineer in our Bible Study also offered to teach some classes and he got the job as well.

I taught a remedial class that took students from addition, subtraction, multiplication and division to pre-algebra. I recall that students who got a low score on a math placement test were required to take this course. I enjoyed teaching there but got tired of teaching the same stuff over and over again. I offered to teach college algebra and calculus but they had full-time instructors that did that. I did finally teach some advanced classes but I got bored and decided not to return for the next semester.

One memorable story comes to mind that readers may enjoy. One day when I was teaching the first session of my remedial math class, I noticed an older lady (40s maybe) in my classroom. She looked out of place since she was older than the typical students and her hair was not well cared for and her body was covered with tattoos. I figured she was some homeless person who wandered into my classroom to get out of the cold.

When I called the roll, she announced her presence and I thought to myself she won't be around long. However, she turned out to be a great student. She came to see me almost every day before class to help her with her homework. As I got to know her, I found out that she had a job welding truck trailers together or some equally lowly job. She was taking my class so she could get a better job, like an indoor job. I saw her one day driving to school in an old 1940s era truck. She apparently did not have a lot of money.

To make a long story short, she got an A in that class and the two courses that followed. I ran into her in a sandwich joint a few years later. She was dressed like a professional. She had a nice dress on and her hair was neatly styled. She told me that she was working in a company with architects. She had her own desk, PC and phone. She was with a well-dressed man who apparently worked with her. We spoke for a while and parted ways. I never saw her again. However, I was happy to see that she got her indoor job after all and she was doing well. Maybe I can take some small amount of credit for helping her achieve her goals. In any case, I was glad I could make some small positive difference in her life.

New Covenant Academy

One day I got a call from New Covenant Academy saying they wanted to start offering some dual credit classes wherein students could get both high school and college credit for the same classes. They asked if I would be willing to teach College Algebra. I agreed because I loved math and algebra was my favorite math course. So I taught a dual credit College Algebra class with Missouri State University. We used the same book as MSU but I could make up my own tests and homework. There was a catch, however. In order to get college credit for the course, my students had to pass the College Algebra final exam. MSU made up the test, MSU graded the test, and MSU gave the test. Lastly, they didn't show me the test until after they gave the test. Nonetheless, my students did remarkably well on the test. In 2010, when I taught my last College Algebra course for NCA, I had ten students. Their scores on the final were 4 A's, 4 B's, 1C and 1 D. No one failed my class. I was delighted.

One day when I was teaching my class, my students came in and told me they were in a math competition the preceding week. Apparently, I was out of school those days. I asked how they did. They replied that two of my students entered the College Algebra competition and they placed first and second. I asked how many students were in the competition. They said 28. I was amazed. The principal was delighted.

On another occasion, I was teaching my class and I noticed one of my students sleeping in class. He did this often. Since he wasn't bothering anyone, I just let him sleep. When the bell rang ending the period, he was still sleeping. So I told my students to please leave the room as quietly as possible which they did. Then I told the incoming students to please enter the room quietly as my student was still sleeping. My daughter Danielle was in the incoming class. That night at dinner, I asked her how long he slept. She said he slept through about half the class and then he woke up in the middle of her Spanish III class. She said he jumped up and left the room. I was hoping this little lesson would cure him of sleeping in my class but, unfortunately, it didn't.

I decided to stop teaching at NCA after Danielle graduated from high school in 2010. I just got tired of always having to be in school every day at a certain time like 10:00 a.m. Even though I only taught for an hour or so, I had to plan my whole day around that hour. So I retired from that job too. Now I occasionally substitute teach math for both New Covenant and Springfield Catholic High School and that's enough for me.

Missouri State University via Internet

MSU started a distance learning program where teachers from MSU would teach high school students from all over the state over the Internet. I interviewed for the job of teaching College Algebra and got it. When I taught my first class, I did it from an office building in Springfield. Then I realized that I could teach it from home. So I sat at my desk with my touchscreen laptop and a headset. The students could see me on their PCs or they could see the blackboard. That was my choice. They could also hear my voice in their classroom. I used the tablet PC like a blackboard and wrote on it and drew diagrams as needed. It worked great and I could teach my class in my pajamas although I never did. I also saved the work I did on my virtual blackboard and put it on the Internet so students who missed class could see everything I did on the board that day.

The concept was great but there was a problem. Many of the remote schools only had a small number of kids who wanted to take the advanced courses like College Algebra. So the MSU virtual school had to combine two or three classes from different schools into one virtual classroom to get the enrollment large enough to have the class. The problem was that the schools were all on different schedules although there was some overlap. So I taught the material when all the schools were present and answered questions and went over homework problems when one or more schools were not online. It worked okay and some of my students did really well, especially on the final. However, some did not do so well. For example, I had a student who was on the golf team and he often missed class due to golf tournaments. When he took the final, he failed the final and the course. So I guess attendance matters after all.

One day I was teaching school A and I noticed a student from school B come online. I asked her if her school was in session that day. She said no but she got online from home to see what was going on in class that day. I was at home and she was at home and the other students were in a classroom and yet we were all together online. When I taught at OTC, students had to drive a long way to come to Springfield to take my classes. On a good day, their commute might be an hour or more. If there was snow or rain, it would be longer. Imagine if I taught all my classes in a virtual setting. Students and teachers do not have to meet in the same room of the same building X times per week. Everyone could join the class from home, or from work, or from their local library, or anywhere else they have Internet access. If the sessions are recorded, they could take the class anytime of the day or night and see and hear the same things that all the other students see and hear. Apparently I was not the only one to realize this. Now my daughter Danielle takes classes at Georgetown University near Washington D.C., from her home in Irvine, California. Isn't technology wonderful? Other than the three hour time difference, the system works fine. The following picture is of me teaching my class from my home office.

Bible Studies

When we moved to Nixa, Missouri we joined a neighborhood Bible Study. We would take turns meeting at each other's houses and reading scripture and answering questions about the readings. My wife Dawn and I really enjoyed these meetings with some very nice Christian people. So while we were still doing these studies, I found out that my church also had a Bible Study so I joined it as well. In my church Bible Study, our first two leaders left after a few years and I became the new leader. So I read all the scripture before we met and wrote discussion questions for our meetings. So far, I wrote questions for the following books of the Bible: Genesis, Exodus, Joshua, Matthew, Mark, Luke, John, Acts of the Apostles, and Revelations.

After all that, I got lazy and started buying books of questions on the books of the Bible but I still led the studies for Judges, 1 Samuel, and Women of the New Testament, comparison of the Passion accounts of Jesus, and the infancy narratives of Jesus in the books of Matthew and Luke.

I am still learning new things about the Bible and plan to continue to study it for the rest of my life.

Apologetics

When I was in that neighborhood Bible Study, I found out that a lot of the things Protestants believe about the Catholic Church are not true. Some of my Protestant neighbors asked me questions about the Catholic Church. I could answer most of their questions but some were things I never heard before. One person told me Peter was not the first pope and he had his reasons for believing that. So I decided to do some research for myself and look into the Catholic Church through the eyes of a non-Catholic Christian. I read several books about Catholicism. I found out a lot of things I didn't know about the Catholic Church.

Then I had another discussion with one of my Protestant friends about the Catholic Church and I felt I did a much better job of defending my faith than I ever did before. So I figured other Catholics might also benefit from learning the things I learned about the church.

So I spoke to our pastor and told him I wanted to teach a course on Apologetics to the members of our parish. He gave me the okay and recommended another guy from our parish as a potential helper for me. His name was Greg Bolda.

I selected a textbook and created six PowerPoint presentations, one for each week of Lent. The presentations basically answered common questions that non-Catholics have about our faith. It also cleared up a lot of misconceptions non-Catholics have about the Catholic Church.

Greg and I taught the class during the six weeks of Lent. We had over thirty people enroll for the first offering and over 50 for the next offering. Feedback from the attendees was encouraging and I expect that I will be doing this for subsequent Lent times or at least until interest in the subject declines. Many people personally thanked Greg and I for doing this class.

CHAPTER 15 MARY BROZOVICH 1916 – 2012

When my father died in 1974, my mother became a widow at age 58. I lived in Woodridge with my wife and three children while my brother and his wife lived in Wisconsin so neither of us was in close proximity with our mother. However, I was closer at about 45 miles away. So I was the one she called when she needed help with anything.

Mom paid her own bills and did her own shopping thanks to her neighbors who took her shopping and brought her home. She went to church daily after my dad died since St. George Church was only two blocks away. She took great care of herself until 1999 when my family and I moved her to Springfield, Missouri about 20 minutes from where we lived.

We found her a duplex she could rent in a senior community called Creekside. The folks who lived there were mostly senior women so she fit right in. Creekside maintained the property so all she had to do was buy her own food and prescription drugs. I took her shopping, paid her bills, balanced her checkbook, took her to doctor appointments, took her with me to church on Sundays, and pretty much did whatever she asked me to do for her. We had a regular lunch date every Wednesday (free pie day at the Village Inn) and Sunday after Mass.

When mom turned 90, we took her with us to a nice place in the Chicago area for dinner and a surprise birthday party. All my kids and grandkids came. Her old neighbors from the East Side also came to celebrate. She was completely surprised and we all had a wonderful time. My mom sat at a table with all her East Side friends and they laughed and talked just like old times. She had a blast.

Another time, Dawn and I took her to Munster, Indiana for the weekend to help her old next door neighbors Mitzie and Eddie celebrate their 50th wedding anniversary. Again she had a great time visiting with them and their family, most of whom she had known for over 50 years.

We also took her with us on numerous occasions to Chicago to see my grandkids and her great grandkids. We drove there and back. The distance was about 500 miles and it took 8 to 10 hours to go one way. No one seemed to mind and we all loved seeing my kids and their kids.

Mom started having medical problems in 2011 so we moved her to the lodge on the Creekside property. There she had a nice one bedroom apartment. All her meals were also provided and she could keep all her Missouri friends. Another big benefit of living there was the restaurant folks would call her if she didn't show up for a meal. Once she fell and they called. When she didn't answer, they found her on the floor and called 9-1-1. They took her to the hospital and they checked her over and told me that everything was ok.

She stayed in her apartment until December of 2011. Then she was having trouble going to the bathroom at night by herself. She was also having problems taking her pills promptly. So we decided to move her to the nursing home on the Creekside property. They could escort her to bathroom whenever she needed help and they also managed her pills for her. She liked it there. Her old Creekside friends came to see her often and she made many new friends in the nursing home. She celebrated her 96th birthday at the nursing home. We all came and had a birthday party for her in the private dining room.

In January of 2012, my mom contracted pneumonia at the nursing home. I spoke to her doctor and he said that if she was younger they could insert a tube in her lungs and drain the fluid out of her lungs. However, they don't do that when a person is 96. So the doctor gave her about three months to live. That's about how long it took for her lungs to fill with fluid until she could no longer breathe.

In the last three months in the nursing home, everybody came to see grandma. All my kids came with their kids. My brother John's kids came and my brother traveled from Washington state to be with her.

On March 15, 2012 my brother and I went to see her. She was in a wheelchair. We took her outside because it was such a beautiful spring day. We just sat outside with her and visited for a while.

JOSEPH BROZOVICH

Everything was very peaceful. I sat on one side of her holding her hand and John did the same on the other side. We didn't plan it that way. It just happened. When we left, we kissed her and said we would see her the following day. That night I got a call from the nursing home saying mom passed away. She was married to my dad for 32 years and she lived alone another 38 years after he died.

We had a wake/visitation for her in Springfield and in Chicago. She was laid to rest next to my dad in Holy Cross Cemetery in Calumet City, Illinois a few days later. Her obituary follows below:

Mary Brozovich | Visit Guest Book

Mary Brozovich

Mary (Peterlich) Brozovich, 96, of Springfield, entered her eternal life on March 15, 2012. Mary was born near Gospic in Lika, Croatia on January 10, 1916. She was preceded in death by her husband, Joe Brozovich, her parents, and 17 brothers and sisters.

Mary is survived by her two sons, Joseph and wife, Dawn, John and wife Celine; nine grandchildren, Joanne, Joyce, Joe and wife Cheryl, Lauren, Amy and husband Manuel, Michael and fiancé Lisa, Faith, John and wife Carla, Danielle; and four great grandchildren, Jose David and Cassandra Duran, Jackson Brozovich and Makayla Brozovich.

Mary was a member of St. Elizabeth Ann Seton Catholic Church. She was best known for her infectious laugh and her award winning apple strudel and walnut bread.

Wake services will begin at 6 p.m., with visitation to follow until 8 p.m., Friday, March 16, 2012 in Herman H. Lohmeyer Funeral Home, 500 E. Walnut Street.

Wake services, funeral mass and burial will be in Chicago, Illinois next week.

Permanent online condolences, stories and photos may be shared at www.hhlohmeyer.com.

CHAPTER 16 LIFE IS ONE BIG CIRCLE

When I was born, I was totally helpless. I couldn't even feed myself. My mom did everything for me. I was the baby and she was the mom. After my Dad died in 1974, my relationship with my mom became one of peers and mom and I became friends. When she moved to Missouri in 1999, she depended on me for almost everything and our relationship evolved into a parent-child relationship except that now I was the parent and she was the child. I suspect our relationship was no different than many others, but it took me awhile to realize what was happening. Then I was glad I could finally help her like she and my dad helped me.

How did my parents help me? First of all, they provided a safe and happy home for me and my brother John to grow up in. Second, they paid for both of us to attend Catholic grammar school and high school. Third, they paid for about half of my college education. My scholarship and summer jobs paid the rest. Fourth, they taught me how to live a good Christian life by words and mostly by example. They taught me to work hard to get ahead in this world. They taught me to save my money to get the things I wanted. They taught me to pay my bills on time and avoid interest charges. My parents loaned me $25,000 to buy my first house. I paid it all back with interest. My mom financed my second house and I paid that all back with interest as well.

Finally, my parents taught me to live my faith in Jesus Christ. Jesus taught us to "Love one another as I have loved you". I always felt that the way we show our love to other people is to be kind to them like in the beatitudes in the Sermon on the Mount in Matthew chapter 5. I feel that God gave each of us special gifts and He gave them to us because He wanted us to use them to help other people. For example, He gave me ability in Math so I became a Math teacher and helped well over a thousand students learn math in high school and college. One mother stopped me after I attended an awards banquet at New Covenant Academy and told me that her daughter got a 27 on the math portion of the ACT before taking my class in College Algebra. The national average is around 21 so she was above average before I ever met her. After taking my class, she got a 34. A perfect score is 35. The 34 score in Math qualified her for a Bright Flight Scholarship which is $2000 per year for up to four years in college. Thanks to her hard work and my help she got her scholarship. Other students I taught also earned this scholarship.

When I went to Catholic high school, the nuns were good teachers and disciplinarians. They knew their stuff and they didn't let us get away with anything. When I was teaching, I tried to help my students learn the subject matter, just like the nuns did for me. Again my life is part of one big circle.

When my brother was planning to go to college, he didn't apply for the scholarship I got from the mill. My parents thought that since I didn't go to work at the mill when I graduated, the mill folks wouldn't give him a scholarship. So they wanted to send him to college but that was a lot of money for them. However, my mom had taken her uncle into our home and let him live in it in his post-retirement years. When he died, he made my mom the beneficiary of his life insurance policy which amounted to $10,000. This was a huge sum of money at that time because they bought their house for less than that. So my mom saved that money until John was ready for college. When the college bills came due, my mom paid them with the life insurance money. As far as I know, she didn't spend a dime of that money on herself. My brother John worked through college and paid some of his own expenses. He also lived at home while attending Purdue University Calumet Campus in Hammond, Indiana. He graduated in four years and went on to get two master's degrees which he funded with his own money. Those were the kind of parents we grew up with. We learned more from watching them than we could have learned any other way. I only hope I did half as well with my own kids.

CHAPTER 17 LETTERS TO JOE

Catholic Retreat in Texas

In 2003, I attended a retreat in San Antonio, Texas. Unbeknownst to me, my brother asked my family members to write letters to me. At the appropriate point in the retreat, the guys making the retreat got to read letters written to them by their family members. These are the letters I got at that retreat. I thanked my kids for writing these letters but I never shared the contents with anyone prior to writing this book. I look at them as upward feedback from my kids on how well I did my job as their parent. Enjoy.

Letter from Joanne

October 8, 2002

Ever since I was a little girl - I respected you as an authority figure, a role model but mostly because you were/are my DAD. I'm so proud of you and our family. I'm proud of what you stand for, how you teach, what you believe and that you challenge status quo. I enjoy telling people about my family, thanks to you, your hard work and many self-sacrifices. It seems so easy to say now looking back, but I know I didn't make it very easy for you or Mom sometimes. I guess I was just a kid trying to find my way, wanting to be accepted and to know that I mattered. Parents have a knack for knowing what's right, especially when it comes to their own children.

I want to say "Thank You" for all the support you've given me over my 35+ years of life. Your kind words of encouragement whenever something was going on - made it just that much easier to believe in myself. It didn't matter if it was a test in grammar school, my 12 years of Spotlight Dance Studio Recitals on Father's Day, a big exam in collage, my summer abroad or my bridges between-employment opportunities— you were right there, pushing me upward with the best attitude I remember when I was sixteen and I was awarded my first traffic citation on Ogden Avenue and how I was so afraid to tell you - I cried all the way home admitting to myself I was about to let you down. After I told you, you made it clear to me that it was a mistake and that there was a lesson to be learned from that humiliating experience. I can laugh now - you were right. Thank You. When I made a bad choice and went on a road trip to NIU with my friends (who weren't enrolled in college courses) you waited up for me and reminded me when I got home what my priorities were, more importantly their order. Thank You. As a result, I was a proud college graduate 4 years later with a Bachelor of Arts Degree with a double major. Most recently, you helped me keep focused on returning to Chicago to be with my boyfriend, family and friends. You sent me the 'Countdown Program" and asked me every time we spoke "how many days left? You helped me to plan long term and to not dwell on the short term, for it too will pass. Dad, even though you have your mom, 6 Kids, a wife and friends, it amazes me that you manage to have time for everyone!!! You're kind and always generous. You've taught me my Christian values that I hope to pass on someday. That going to Mass every weekend is just because and not an option. You taught me the difference between right and wrong, good and bad, hot and cold. You taught me to live within my means, to be careful but not afraid. Obviously some lessons were easier taught than others. Dad, your spark in sharing excitement shines through all the time. I recall a brown paper towel in my baby book - the message you wrote when Mom was in labor, anticipating your first-born child - ME. The way you wrote smiled as you spelled IT'S A GIRL!!" Life has a way of whispering to us when sacred moments are occurring. Dad, I still depend on you, obviously not as much because you taught me to be self-sufficient.

You taught me how to have friends which is to be a friend first - listen, be genuine and honest, offer advice when asked, but mostly listen. Thank you. I've stepped away from childhood, away from innocence, away from our home where you protected me and into my own with a good foundation and common sense. I remember my first days of school - with new clothes and fully loaded school bags -- you taking pictures of the 3 Musketeers (me, Joyce and Joe) in front of the bush at the bottom of the driveway. I recall the big world of blackboards, new pencils, and knowledge to be had. You may have forgotten, but I was the first student in the 3 grade to be allowed to use pen on my assignments because I had exceptional handwriting. I remember you helping me move out into my first apartment - driving loads of stuff over to Green Trails and helping me to get settled into my first apartment. Oh how fun that was - a family affair!!!

As I got older and nearer to that magical day, I think about my first step down the aisle with you at my side, gleaming as brightly as I. I think about my youth, purity and your arm entwined in mine. My hands full of beautiful flowers, my heart full of hopes and promises. Down the aisle we'll step - holding on tight as you have in the past, and then releasing my hand and taking the hand of a young man to whom you would entrust a most precious treasure --- your daughter. I'd love to push the PAUSE button on life and freeze our most memorable days. However, life isn't like that. Those who love life must love it with open hands and hearts. We must release time and save only the memories. We must remember that with each first step comes a new journey of joy, surprises, and gentle whispers of God's presence. Please do your best to stay nearby, if only in spirit. I love your phone calls by the way. I ask you this, if I fall, please help me up; if I stumble, please try to catch me. And should my steps lead me astray, please redirect me towards God's path. I know that should I ever grow weary of walking, or fearful into stepping into the shadows or just need to stop and see if I'm aimed in the right direction, I know you'll be there.   -

Without a doubt, you've made it quite clear that should any pain, evil or even hell itself, would have to deal with you before it could get to your precious family.

I Love You Dad,

Thanks for everything and being YOU.

Annie

Letter from Joyce

Oct 8, 2002

Dear Dad,

I wanted to write you a letter of thanks for all of the good things in my life that I have attributed to you.

First of all, I want to say thanks for instilling in me at a young age that I have a higher power that can turn to when things get rough. You gave me a religious gift that only a father and mother can give.

Secondly sending me to private school helped me to become a more sympathetic person as well as I believe a more tolerant person. You also gave me the stepping stones that I needed in high school when I thought that I could not pass that hard class or the time when you came to the school when I was having problems with my peers. I also remember a time when you knew better than I did that I needed someone to take care of me in a way that you couldn't. When I was hospitalized in my sophomore year for example. In addition, thank you for believing in me when I thought that there was no way that I could go back to college. And look at me now, I will be graduating this spring!!!!!

As well as teaching me my religious beliefs, you also taught me right from wrong and good from bad. I also want to thank you for the times when I got that spanking that was well deserved because, I believe that made me a better person in the long run. You also taught me about money and even helped me out when I needed you the most.

You also have an enormous amount of faith in all of us kids that we are outstanding human beings no matter what path we choose to follow in our lives.

In conclusion, you are not only my father but also my role model. I saw that you worked hard for us as a family and only wanted the best for all of us and I cannot thank you enough for all your hard work and dedication!!!!! I know deep in my heart that I can always count and trust in you!!

Love Always,

Twin #1 Joyce Ann

Letter from Son Joe

October 9, 2002

Father,

It would be impossible to convey the thoughts one has for his father in an email, so I will highlight a couple of thoughts that came to mind.

I like many others consider imitation to be the sincerest form of flattery. That said, many people have often compared me to you and in a favorable light. I can't think of another person I would most like to be compared to (sans your most limited food palette) of course.

At a very young age you instilled in me a sense of self-dependence that I carry forward to this day. When I assist others with household tasks varying from light electrical work to automotive work I am amazed at how much you have taught me. Whenever a complement is bestowed upon me for my "expertise", I am quick to promote you as the source of my skills. I look forward to a day when I can pass my knowledge on to my children. It must be incredibly gratifying to see your children succeed and to know that you have played a major role in that success.

Another ideal you instilled upon all of your children at a very young age is the emphasis on education. You selflessly offered all of your children the finest education possible. At some point in your life you tirelessly worked two jobs two be the "best provider you could be. The education you provided us has enabled us to excel at our daily endeavors and for that we are eternally grateful.

As I continue you to grow as a person I come to appreciate the finer things in life. I have never been one who emphasizes possessions, but rather less tangible things like honesty, candor, and leadership. The honesty and candor I express to others has served me well in life and these are traits I trace back to you. You have always demonstrated leadership by quiet example and I include myself as one of your devout followers.

I wish you well in that which you seek at this retreat and I certainly hope that my thoughts will reinforce what others have said. While I will never be able to sign the name as legibly as you, I feel honored to bare the same name as my father.

Your son,

Joe Brozovich

Letter from Amy

Dear Dad,

I can only say thanks. You have been such an important part of my life, I don't know where to start I suppose the earliest, clearest memory I have is of us in Mrs. Shives' first grade classroom at Saint Joan of Arc School. I can remember us dancing at the Father-Daughter dance and all I could think was "That's my dad." That pride has been in the depths of my soul from such a young age. From the encouraging winks while on stage with the Spotlight Studio dance troops to the first videotaped family affair of my First Communion, your motivating smile and words have molded me in so many ways.

Though all the kids could probably say the same, I have always felt like the apple of your eye. I was the one who got a ride to school in high school, and it was never any trouble for you to wake up a half hour earlier to get me there on time, and yourself to work at a decent hour. I was the one who was privileged enough to take the Bonneville to my high school dances. I was the one you walked down the aisle at the end of this summer. I wish I knew the words that could best express my feelings of unconditional love, respect and trust a love that I have only found in our relationship.

There is nothing like a father who you can talk to about anything, a father who would never say that he is too busy or too broke to help you out. Though I may not have made all the right decisions in my life thus far, I have never felt, for even a second, that I was not everything you wanted me to be. You have accepted my faults and helped me accept them as well. Your continuous support will be a part of me forever.

Through my many struggles, you often shed light. One example I still share with friends Is this: One Saturday night I was getting ready to go dancing with my girlfriends, and my Jeans were tighter than usual, I asked what you thought and you said, "Amy, there are girls who would die to look as good as you!" Though we laughed it off then, I often go back to that day and say to myself, "there are still girls who would die to look like me."

In my struggles with Corporate America, I often seek your advice, especially when dealing with others. I now know and continue to remind myself that "Not everyone thinks like me." I might think that day, they are looking to make me mad or they are idiots, but in remembering your philosophy, I am forced to revisit patience and the unconditional acceptance of others.

In the growth of my family, I want to say thank you for your patience. I know that Manuel will never provide for me the way you did, but he and I will make it together. I know in your accepting Manuel you forfeited your dreams for me, but soon after you realized my happiness. In my eyes, this has been the ultimate sacrifice that you have made for me. Having a son of my own, I can't imagine how difficult it would be for me to let go of all the dreams I have for him, since he now is the apple of my eye.

Overall, I would like to say thanks for all that you have contributed to my life and I hope that in return, I have become the daughter that you wanted me to be.

Love Always,

Your Amy Boz

Letter from Michael

Dear Dad,

I want to take this opportunity to say thanks. I only wish that there was a bigger word to express the way I feel. But thanks are the only way I can say it. So here it goes. I want to say thanks that you, mom, and Dawn raised me, for instilling in me the work ethics that you did. Thank you for being a good example by going to work every day, putting food on our table, and still being there when we needed you. Thank you for always being ready and willing to help out with whatever problems we brought to you.

I also want to thank you for teaching me about respect and love. These qualities molded me into the young "gentleman" I feel I am today because of your advice and actions on how to treat people as I would want to be treated. Even though we didn't always agree, you still stood behind me in everything I did and showed me how to learn from my mistakes and how to capitalize on my achievements. For example, supporting myself at eighteen, becoming a leader in my new occupation, treating Lisa like the precious girl she is, and making peace with Dawn after so long.

On behalf of all the kids, thanks for being dad.

Love always,
your youngest son

Mike

Letter from Dawn

October 9, 2002

Dear Joe,

I hope that you are enjoying the retreat and time with your brother. I'm really glad that you were able to take time away for yourself. You are a wonderful and caring husband and you deserve this time! It seems like you are always caring for or working for someone else: your Mom, me, Danielle or even one of the other kids. Now, you have a few days to concentrate on yourself; and on what is good for you!

You are a wonderful man, Joe! I am so lucky to be married to you! When I listen to others talk about their spouse it seems like no one is as happy as I am. We just "click". Even if we disagree on something, which happens so seldom that I think I could count those things on one hand, we listen to each other and try to understand the other person. You make me feel accepted and loved, just the way I am. What a wonderful feeling!

You are also a wonderful son! You really have a way of being understanding, patient, and loving toward your Mom. I realize that seems like something that's very natural to you, but believe me, many sons are not able to put into words and actions something that you do so naturally!

Last, but not least... You are a wonderful father! You have five grown who have turned out terrific. They have become responsible, independent adults who enjoy being with each other and with us. Each of them is different, but you love them all the same! Danielle is growing to be a lovely young lady as well.

I'm glad that you are getting a chance to reconnect with your brother. I know that you have really missed having a close relationship with him in the past. I'm glad to see that you have been able to rekindle that closeness with him. I'm also glad that you are available to support him during this difficult time in his life.

Thanks for all of your love and devotion these past 12+ years. They have been the most wonderful years of my life!

I love you!

Dawn

Letter from My Brother John

October 29, 2004

Dear Joe,

Thank you for being who you are. I am grateful you are my brother. And, I am delighted we have gotten closer to God through be available to each other.

You have always been a shining light of example to me. Thank you for everything you are and have been to me throughout my life.

I am excited for your involvement on the ACTS team this weekend. You make a difference to everyone you meet by being who you are. You're authentic. You are intelligent. You are a good listener. You have an even keel. You are a student and teacher of the Bible. It has been very special to see you and experience you grow in your knowledge of the Bible.

God Bless You, Joe.

Your brother,

John

Letter 2 from My Brother John

10-5-02

Dear Joe,

You've always been there for me as my big brother. You helped me with math and I remember learning calculus from you at Uncle Jim's house one night. You took the time to be there and offer yourself to me intellectually and as a brother in Christ.

The April ACTS retreat for me was a turning point. I needed it and I didn't even know it. I have made a sincere effort to put God first in my life and rid myself of anger. It has been six months and I have a life I am very close to God in a relationship like never before.

Only you know what you need in your relationship with God. You are a blessing to the world. May this retreat renew your relationship with God in a way that advances your highest self.

You have always been a role model to me. You are a brilliant person with a deep

I am so glad God gave you to me as a brother. You are an inspiration by your calm steadfast ways. I am here to serve you in the retreat. It is a joy to be of service to you. Thank you for allowing me to be here by accepting the invitation to participate.

God Bless you, Joe.

Love

Your brother, John

Letter from My Mom (written by John)

Oct. 5, 02

Dear loving son Joe,

I appreciate so much everything you do for me. And, I love you so much for it. I am happy you are on this retreat in Texas. You deserve it. I am thinking about you and praying for you as you participate in the ACTS retreat.

You have always been a good Catholic man. I am proud that you and your family are close to God. I pray you will continue to discover a close relationship with God. I pray for you always.

Blessings and Love,
Your Mom,

Mary Brozovich

CHAPTER 18 JOE RETIRES

Planning for Retirement

While I was still working I heard a story about a pension-eligible employee. They were having a service anniversary party for him and people were asking him when he was going to retire. He said he couldn't afford to retire. He needed his income to live. So he and his manager sat down and did some calculations. The first thing they did was subtract his pension from his salary because now he was working for difference between the two. They also subtracted his estimated Social Security income. Then they divided the remaining amount by the number of hours he worked. This calculation showed that he was working for about one dollar per hour. He would be money ahead by retiring and getting a minimum wage job. The man couldn't believe it. He said he was going to home and figure it out for himself. The next day when he arrived at work, he marched into his manager's office and said "I retire".

Since I didn't want this to be my story too, I started planning for my retirement in the 1980s when I got my first home mortgage paid off. I was constantly calculating my expected pension and my net worth. By the 1990s, Dawn and I were planning to retire to Missouri because the cost of living was less than Illinois and the home prices were a lot less.

To accomplish our goal of retiring early we were saving money every way we knew how. We increased our contributions to our company savings plans as much as we could.

In the 1990s my annual pay increases came in two parts: an increase in my base pay and a bonus. I asked all my managers to give me 0% increase in pay and give me the maximum bonus they could. I did this because the big bonus was part of my pension calculation. A pay increase was also a factor, but I was not planning to be there long enough to collect my increased pay for very long. So my managers accepted my proposal. I got 0% pay increases and large bonuses my last few years. This helped me and it also made more salary money available for the young people who would be collecting their pay increases for many years. Plus their future raises would be calculated on a larger salary base. So it was a win – win for everyone.

My goal was to retire by age 55. The only drawback to this plan was that I would not be eligible for Social Security until I reached my full retirement age of 65 or 66 although I would be eligible for a reduced social security benefit at age 62. If I took SS at age 62, I would collect less money than a person retiring at age 66. However, I would collect the lower payment for 4 years more than the guy retiring at 66 who got his increased amount. I figured it would take the other guy to age 84 to catch up with me in total social security benefits. I could live with that.

Retiring early also meant that I could not collect Medicare benefits until I reached 65. So there was a 10 year gap when I was responsible for paying the health insurance premiums for me, Dawn and Danielle. All the other kids were gone by the time I retired.

Healthcare costs surprised me. My first year of retirement, my healthcare premium was $17 per month. This was pocket change. Lunch could cost more than that.

The next year it went up to $50 per month. This didn't seem too bad. The following year, it went up to $150 dollars per month. I didn't like where this was going.

The next year my monthly premium went to $450 per month. This was getting out of control. The shrewd reader should realize by now that the premium was tripling every year. By the following year the premium went up to almost $1000 per month. This was exorbitant. Now I started looking for healthcare plans outside of my company plan. I finally did cancel the company healthcare plan and got my own private insurance plan and it stayed at around $900 per month for several years.

As my healthcare premiums were increasing, my pension stayed the same. It never went up by one red cent. Since my healthcare premiums were increasing annually, my pension checks were reduced by the amount of my healthcare premiums.

The good news was that my income did go up when I started collecting Social Security. At this time both Dawn and I were working part-time. Dawn was doing taxes at a small CPA firm in Springfield and I was teaching at some local colleges so we were not hurting for money.

Joe's Third Family Grows Up

When I first got married and had children. My family consisted of MaryAnne, Joanne, Joyce, Joe and myself. We were a happy family of five. About 10 years after Joanne was born, Amy came on the scene with Michael to follow about two and a half years later.

Shortly after Michael was born, the older kids started high school and got jobs after school. By now, they were getting pretty independent. At this point we were raising our second family consisting of MaryAnne, Amy, Michael and me.

When we moved to Missouri in 1998, we began raising my third family consisting of Dawn, Danielle and me. We were in a new house in a new city and a new state. We didn't know anyone except for Dawn's mom who lived about 40 miles away from us. So our little family of three started our new life in Nixa, Mo. In 1999 we moved my mom to Springfield so we were not alone any more.

When we lived in Nixa, Missouri, Danielle got involved in sports. She played basketball and soccer. Danielle and I had a standing date every day after school. We would play one on one basketball on our driveway since the previous owners left us a basketball hoop there. We played until Dawn called us in for dinner. Danielle got pretty good even if I couldn't teach her much. The first basketball team she played on won the championship in their little universe. The coach made a video tape of their season to commemorate the event. We still have it.

As we had to take Dani to all her practices and games, we got to meet lots of new people who were doing the same things for their kids. We also got to meet our neighbors when we joined a small neighborhood bible study.

Danielle's Academic Story

When we were in Chicago, Danielle attended a Montessori school which she really liked. The interesting thing about her class was that she was in the minority. Out of 23 students in her class, only five were Caucasians. Nonetheless she loved it and learned a lot. So when we came to Missouri, they put her in kindergarten because she had just turned six. However, she was bored out of her mind. So we spoke to her teacher and told them about her previous school and the things she did. They agreed to test her. The day after the test, they said they would move her into first grade. So she skipped the second half of kindergarten.

Then, at the end of the year, the teachers asked us if we wanted them to hold her back because she was the youngest kid in her class and she always would be if she didn't go back. We made it clear that she mastered the material and we wanted her to go to second grade. So she went on to second grade and we never regretted our decision.

After attending first, second and third grade at the Nixa public school, we were disappointed that Danielle was not getting much homework and the classes were proceeding very slowly. On one occasion I asked Danielle what she learned in school that day and she said "Nothing." I said "You were there all day. How could you learn nothing? What did you do for seven hours?" She said they reviewed. I asked if they did that all day and she said yes. I asked why. She said the teachers cannot go to new material until the majority of the class masters the subject matter. She got it the first time while others struggled.

We talked to her teacher about it and she told us the same thing that Danielle did. We said "We both have our master's degrees and we expect the same for Danielle." She said that the school was pleased when most of the students can graduate from high school. It was then and there that we decided to find a more appropriate school for Danielle.

The following year, we enrolled Danielle in New Covenant Academy in Springfield Mo. NCA was a small private Christian school for grades K through 12. Danielle started in 4th grade. She liked NCA. She had homework every night and she could participate in anything she wanted. Since it was a small school, they needed students for all the activities. If a student asked to be in a given activity, they were in. Danielle chose to participate in basketball, band, and volleyball.

When Danielle was near the end of her first year at NCA, they had an honors assembly. Danielle got a certificate for Teacher's Honor Roll for kids with all A's and B's. Some kids got Principal's Honor Roll certificates meaning they got all A's. After the assembly was over, we congratulated Danielle on her accomplishment. As we walked out of the gym, she crumpled up her certificate and threw it in the trash saying "That will never happen again". And she got all A's ever since.

While attending high school at NCA, Danielle got involved in Bible Quiz at her church. This is where kids memorize books of the Bible and compete with other kids to answer questions on the book(s) they memorized. Yes you read that right. She memorized entire books of the Bible. She memorized the book of Acts of the Apostles and the Gospel of Mark in consecutive years. She competed on a team at her church and at the end of her senior year, she and her team went to a national competition in Troy, Michigan. Her team finished 5th out of 40 teams and she had the 8th highest individual score out of about 150 quizzers.

Danielle thrived at NCA. She stayed there all the way through high school. She graduated in 2010 as one of three valedictorians of her class. After leaving NCA, she decided to go to Evangel University. Evangel is a small private Christian college in Springfield.

In the summer of 2009, Danielle needed to do an internship as part of her degree program. So big sister Joanne got her a job at Electromotive Diesel in LaGrange, Illinois. Danielle stayed with Joanne and they carpooled to work together for her 10 week internship. Danielle had a great time living in the Chicago area. She went to a Cubs game, ate real Chicago pizza, and went to downtown Chicago and many other places. She also got to visit with her siblings and all her nieces and nephews.

In June of 2014, she graduated Summa Cum Laude with her bachelor's degree in Finance. After graduating, she couldn't find a job in Springfield so she moved to Chicago and continued her job search while living with big sister Joanne. That summer she got a job with Deloitte in downtown Chicago.

In 2015, Danielle started pursuing her master's degree in Finance from Georgetown University in Washington D.C. via Internet. She left Deloitte in October, 2016 to concentrate on finishing her master's degree. She graduates in May of 2017.

Danielle's Basketball Exploits

Danielle's team was playing a bigger and more physical team on Thursday, Dec. 11, 2005. During the course of the game, Danielle played every position, as she had done in the last three games. She scored five points and got several rebounds and assists. With a little over two minutes left in the game and the other team in the lead, the star of the other team broke away for a layup. Danielle stood stock still in front of the basket with her hands straight up in the air. The girl could have gone to either side of Danielle, but she chose to jump right into Danielle as she made her layup. The girl should have been called for a charge, her 5th and final foul, the basket should not have counted and Danielle should have gone to the free throw line (All this according to a person in the audience who is a certified basketball referee.) What actually happened was Danielle was called for a blocking foul and the basket counted and the girl got a free throw as well. When Danielle tumbled to the floor with the girl on top of her, she must have put her hand down to break her fall. She said her right hand went numb after the fall. Dawn took her to the ER and they said she may have a fracture in one of the bones in her right wrist. We took her to an orthopedic surgeon the following week to get a more accurate diagnosis.

Although we lost the game, this was perhaps the best game Danielle played all year. Many people in the crowd came up to Danielle after the game and congratulated her on her fine game. They also cheered her name when she made several fine plays during the course of the game. In one play, a player from the other team broke away for a basket. Danielle caught up to her from behind as she was going in for a layup, blocked the layup and took the ball away from her. She did all this without committing a foul. Needless to say, I was the proudest dad in the school that night.

Joe Meets Ike Crawford and Bobby Bostic

One day in the fall of 2011, I found a letter at the South Side Senior center where I played chess addressed to the president of the chess club. Since I was the president, I opened the letter. It was from a man in prison wanting to play a postal game of chess where we mail moves back and forth to play the game. I sent a letter back to him and agreed to play a game with him. At first I had him send his moves to the senior center but as I got to know him, I gave him my home address. Our first game went on for months but I finally won it.

While we were exchanging letters, he told me his story of how he ended up in prison. Basically, he and two friends went to a McDonald's restaurant to get some food. They were jumped by three other guys in the restaurant. The other guys got the better of Ike and his friends and beat and robbed Ike. After the beating and robbery, one of Ike's friends produced a gun and gave it to Ike. He went back into the restaurant and demanded that the guys who beat and robbed him return the stuff they stole from him. One thing led to another and he shot and killed two of them. He was only 17 years old. A few days later Ike gave himself up to the police. He was tried and convicted of murder and given a life sentence without parole in an adult maximum security prison. When he started writing to me, he had been in prison for about 20 years.

Over the next several years we got to be good friends and I even went to visit him in prison in Licking, Mo. In those years, there were several court cases that decided that incarcerating youths under 18 a life sentence without parole violated the eight amendment of the U.S. constitution regarding cruel and unusual punishment. To make a long story short, Ike and people like him will be eligible for parole after serving 25 years. Ike will have 25 years in prison in 2017. Ike's parole hearing will occur sometime in 2017.

While talking to Ike, he introduced me to another life without parole person named Bobby Bostic. Bobby was 16 years old in 1995 when he and an older man committed the robbery of two people who were in a crowd of five people and committed another robbery of a single individual thirty minutes later a few blocks away. No one was seriously injured in these crimes but Bobby was sentenced to 241 years in prison for these crimes.

Bobby asked me to send out letters to people trying to convince people that he got a bad deal being sentenced to 241 years in prison at the age of 16. I sent an email to a reporter for the St. Louis Post Dispatch and she wrote an article about Bobby and men in similar situations. His article appeared on the front page of the Sunday edition of the St. Louis Post Dispatch on Aug. 10, 2014.

Some people ask me why I got involved with such people. I tell them about Matthew 25:36 which says: "[36] I was naked and you clothed me, I was sick and you visited me, I was in prison and you came to me." I never thought I would ever meet anyone in prison but I did and I interpret that to mean that God made it happen so I could help these folks and that is what I am doing.

EPILOGUE

The Brozovich Family Today

As the year 2016 winds to a close, a look at our current family shows our original six children plus seven grandchildren. Amy and Manuel have Jose David, Cassandra and Mary Grace. Michael and Lisa brought us Makayla, Emily and Aria. Joe and Cheryl have Jackson. All of the family members are doing well.

Now Grandpa Joe and Grandma Dawn are enjoying life traveling all over the United States with their joint goal of visiting all the states. So far, they have each visited about 47 of the 50 states. Vermont and Rhode Island will get checked off in 2017 and Joe will only have North Dakota on his bucket list. Dawn needs New Jersey and Connecticut to finish her bucket list.

This year I celebrated my 72nd birthday. As I look back on my 72 years on this planet, I feel pretty happy. Thanks to my parents, I got a great Catholic school education which prepared me for my successful matriculation at Purdue University, and the Illinois Institute of Technology.

I married two wonderful women and had six great kids. All my kids are college graduates except Michael but I knew college was not for him and Michael is a huge success even without a degree.

I had a great career at Western Electric, AT&T, and Lucent Technologies and retired as a Distinguished Member of the Technical Staff, an honor not achieved by most engineers. I had the privilege of working with some very smart people and we achieved the distinction of getting a U.S. patent on the Emergency 9-1-1 system in use in Chicago and other cities throughout the country. I fully expect that system to work well and evolve in the future and save lives by delivering the emergency calls to the call center faster than ever before.

My second career in teaching has also been a joy to me. I have seen my students grow up and become mature and responsible adults. Many have thanked me for helping them succeed in the courses I taught. I have seen people go from lowly minimum wage jobs to successful professionals.

I am eternally grateful to God for giving me the opportunity to retire early and be able to spend more time with my wife and daughter and studying his word through Bible Studies and small groups at my church.

I worked almost 33 years as an engineer. My goal is to be retired at least that long. So far I have been retired for almost 18 years (since March, 1999). I am hoping God gives me another 15 years so I can see some of my great grandchildren grow up.

The picture below was taken at my 70th birthday party with Dawn, all my kids, their spouses, and all the grand kids.

Someday, when my time on this earth runs out, I hope to see Jesus waiting for me at the gates of heaven with my mom, dad and all my deceased friends and family members saying "Well done good and faithful servant".

Joe's 70th Birthday Party

ABOUT THE AUTHOR

Joe Brozovich is the Average Joe. He was born in the 1940s and grew up in the 50s and 60s on the southeast side of Chicago with his parents and his brother, John. He earned his bachelor's degree in Electrical Engineering from Purdue University in 1966 and his master's degree in Electrical Engineering from the Illinois Institute of Technology in 1971. He worked for Western Electric/AT&T/Lucent Technologies for almost 33 years where primary job was inventing new things. In 1994, Joe and his team mates were awarded a U.S. patent for a new type of 9-1-1 Public Safety Answering Point that delivered 9-1-1 calls to the 9-1-1 call takers faster than any other previous technology.

Joe was married twice and had six children and they blessed him with seven grandchildren. Most of his family lives in the Chicago suburbs. Joe and his wife retired to southwestern Missouri. It was here that Joe embarked on his second career, teaching College Algebra to high school and college students.

When Joe finally left his second career, Joe felt compelled to share his story with his children and grandchildren. Average Joe is his story. It answers the question, "What did grandpa do when he was a kid like us?"

Made in the USA
Monee, IL
15 October 2024

67854106R10063